YOUR BEST YOU
HOW TO WORK
WHAT YOU'VE GOT
TO LOOK GREAT
EVERY DAY

SONYA LENNON &

BRENDAN COURTNEY

YOUR
HOW TO WORK WHAT YOU'VE
BEST
GOT TO LOOK GREAT EVERY DAY
YOU

GILL & MACMILLAN

TO LAUNDRY ROOM
THANK YOU FOR ALL YOUR SUPPORT OVER THE
YEAR. ALSO, TO THE TIRELESS FASHION ASSISTANTS
AND INTERNS THAT OIL THE MACHINE, AND TO OUR
BRILLIANT HAIR AND MAKE-UP TEAM.

GILL & MACMILLAN
HUME AVENUE, PARK WEST
DUBLIN 12
WITH ASSOCIATED COMPANIES
THROUGHOUT THE WORLD
WWW.GILLMACMILLANBOOKS.IE

© SONYA LENNON AND BRENDAN COURTNEY 2012
ISBN: 978 07171 5393 0
DESIGN BY WWW.GRAHAMTHEW.COM
PHOTOGRAPHY BY PETER ROWEN
CAPSULE BRA SHOTS (P. 57), SUPPORT UNDERWEAR
SHOTS (P. 51), MOOD BOARD (P. 23) AND RACHEL WALSH,
SANCTUM (P. 115), PHOTOGRAPHED BY AARON MCGRATH.
PRINTED BY GRAPHYCEMS, SPAIN

THIS BOOK IS TYPESET IN 11 POINT NEUTRA TEXT BOOK.
THE PAPER USED IN THIS BOOK COMES FROM THE WOOD
PULP OF MANAGED FORESTS. FOR EVERY TREE FELLED,
AT LEAST ONE TREE IS PLANTED, THEREBY RENEWING
NATURAL RESOURCES.

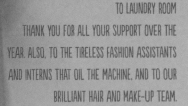

CONTENTS

INTRODUCTION

IT'S HARD TO BELIEVE that it's been three years since our last book. As we have worked our way steadily through seven seasons of *Off The Rails*, our experience has helped us to fine-tune our message. We know the burning style and image questions that need answering. We know the body hang-ups that stop us from enjoying the best of ourselves. We know the style conundrums, from school gate to boardroom. We know, because you tell us. Everywhere we go, women approach us with personal style queries, 'What shape am I?', 'What size bra should I be wearing?' We stop and chat and discuss the issues at hand. Sometimes in a dedicated workshop, sometimes in the supermarket. Often women say, 'I wish I could get a makeover on *Off The Rails* – but I wouldn't go on the telly wearing that body suit!'

Well, now you can have the burning style questions answered in *Your Best You*.

Our inspiration in writing this book has been you – real women with busy lives. At least one of us (no prizes for guessing which one) knows what it's like to be a busy mum. Women are the world's best jugglers. Not only do many of us work outside the home, we are also often at the forefront of the home, too – and when we're not there in person, we're always there in spirit, managing the logistics of it all.

A very successful businesswoman shared her experience with us, saying, 'I asked my husband if, when he was at work, he yearned for our kids, if he longed to be with them and if he constantly battled with himself about whether being away from them was the right thing to do. "Em, not really," he replied.' Sound familiar?

#YOURBESTYOU

ASK YOURSELF:

ARE THERE BITS OF YOUR BODY THAT DRIVE YOU MAD?

DO YOU FIND SHOPPING A CAUSE FOR ANXIETY?

ARE YOU HAPPY WITH THE CLOTHES YOU OWN?

DO YOU FEEL THAT HOW YOU LOOK REPRESENTS WHO YOU REALLY ARE?

ARE YOU CONFIDENT ABOUT HOW YOU LOOK?

IF YOUR ANSWER IS YES TO THE FIRST TWO AND NO TO THE REST, YOU'VE COME TO THE RIGHT PLACE!

Frankly, women take on a lot, whether you work outside the home or not; very easy to lose yourself in the mayhem. Then one day you look in the mirror and you recognise neither the body nor the woman looking at you. It can be a scary moment, and is as likely to happen at 30 as it is at 40 and 50 and 60 and 70. But the good news is that help is at hand and you *can* regain that self-confidence that's so much a part of you and your personal style.

A gorgeous makeover candidate on *Off The Rails* once said, 'All I want is for someone to tell me I look great and for me to honestly say that I just threw it on.'

Having great style means that you look self-assured and effortless, that you have that elusive sense of yourself and an understanding of your true beauty. Makes it sound almost romantic, doesn't it?

However, as we all know, it's not that easy. Doing something really well, from dancing to pole-vaulting, takes investment. But investment doesn't have to mean money. The investment we're talking about comes in the form of understanding, knowledge and application. In other words, a little bit of effort. But the good news is, we're here to help. In *Your Best You*, we'll show you how to look your best and maximize your confidence. We believe that all women want to feel confident about how they look, regardless of the style direction that they take.

So how is this book going to help you to crack your own personal style and fly into a new-found confidence about how you look? Well, we have the knowledge and experience to impart, but guess what? You hold the key. The gorgeous girls who volunteered to be in this book have been specially chosen to represent the different body shapes of the Irish woman, but this book is about you, and the steps that you can take towards becoming your best you. What we've developed in *Your Best You* is a self-assessment guide, so that you can apply our process to your own lifestyle, to get a clear and defined picture of what you are, in body-shape terms, but also, who you are, in lifestyle terms. When you are clear and honest about these two things, you can then begin to develop a wardrobe designed especially for your needs and finally learn how to become, *Your Best You*. And it'll be fun — we promise . . .

Along the way, we will ask you to make some notes, nothing too difficult: just a few observations. These notes will help you to understand your own style needs, and ensure that all your future choices are as informed as possible.

So what will that mean in real terms?

Although this is definitely a book you can dip in and out of (we know you've already skipped to chapter 2 to see what body shape you are!) we strongly encourage you to read it as it's written. It will help you to get the most out of it and really see permanent effects.

But of course, we couldn't have done it without you. From those of you whose burning style questions gave us the inspiration to write this book, to our gorgeous makeover gals, and in a new twist, the women who feature in our Celebration of Real Beauty. Here, we asked you to submit stories and pictures of your loved ones whom you feel epitomise *real* beauty. Women who you feel deserve to be celebrated. We scheduled a fabulous photo shoot and gave them a great day of glamour and pampering. We asked them to tell us why they felt beautiful then we catalogued the day through pictures which are featured throughout this book as a celebration of real beauty.

We're adamant that we want you to have the best possible experience with this book and ultimately to get the best possible results — so with this in mind, we encourage you to go on-line and find us both on Facebook and Twitter and then feel free to ask us any question you like. If you get stuck or find any part of the book and journey too challenging, we are only a click away. Let this book be the catalyst to becoming your best you. Because doing and being *your* best is all you can do.

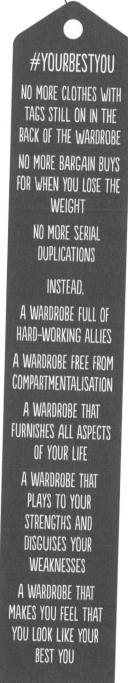

#YOURBESTYOU

NO MORE CLOTHES WITH TAGS STILL ON IN THE BACK OF THE WARDROBE

NO MORE BARGAIN BUYS FOR WHEN YOU LOSE THE WEIGHT

NO MORE SERIAL DUPLICATIONS

INSTEAD,

A WARDROBE FULL OF HARD-WORKING ALLIES

A WARDROBE FREE FROM COMPARTMENTALISATION

A WARDROBE THAT FURNISHES ALL ASPECTS OF YOUR LIFE

A WARDROBE THAT PLAYS TO YOUR STRENGTHS AND DISGUISES YOUR WEAKNESSES

A WARDROBE THAT MAKES YOU FEEL THAT YOU LOOK LIKE YOUR BEST YOU

CHAPTER 1

WHO ARE YOU TODAY?

TAKE A LOOK AT YOUR LIFESTYLE

OUR CLOTHES PROVOKE VERY STRONG EMOTIONS IN US. HOW YOUR WARDROBE AFFECTS YOU BECOMES PRETTY CLEAR THE MINUTE YOU OPEN THOSE DOORS.

DO YOU LOOK AT YOUR sartorial choices and think, So many great looks, what am I going to wear? If so, chances are you are completely happy and in control of your image or have a personal stylist.

For the majority of us, the reality is something very different: the doors open accompanied by a sigh of dissatisfaction. There are lots of items hanging there, and yet nothing to wear.

Do you have items in your wardrobe with tags still on? If so, you're not alone, so many women suffer from this guilty secret. Often, it's down to the lure of the bargain. 'How could I possibly leave it?' you ask, 'It's down from €250 to €50!' or, '€25 to €5'. Well, you need to ask yourself a couple of key questions here. Firstly, why is there such a reduction? Secondly, do you want it because it's a 'bargain' or because it's right for you and your lifestyle?

Do you have special-occasion 'outfits', the dreaded 'rig-outs' (which are not cheap!) hanging limply in your wardrobe having had one moment of glory, only to find that the photographic evidence shows a worrying delusion on your part! Working on the basis of *price per wear* (e.g., if you buy a dress that costs €200 and wear it twenty times, that's €10 per wear) these flights of fancy can be expensive if they end up as museum pieces. Particularly when we are prepared to spend so much less on our casual wear, which may well represent what we wear the most.

So, what do you want your wardrobe to do for you? Wouldn't it be nice to be able to open those doors and see faithful friends beaming at you in delight, joyfully exclaiming, 'Pick me, pick me!' In this Shangri La, style solutions abound for the many sides of you: the go-getting businesswoman, the stylish school-run mum, the girl running down to the shops (but still looking great) and the diva that sashays out to dinner to gasps of admiration from all, young and old. It would be great to know that you had every style possibility covered in your wardrobe, wouldn't it?

Let's assume your goal is to change your approach to your personal style, and in so doing, gain more confidence about how you look. In order to do this, you must really understand *Who You Are*, in terms of your lifestyle and *What you Are*, in terms of

#YOURBESTYOU
A REALLY USEFUL TIP FOR AVOIDING BARGAIN MISTAKES IS TO SIMPLY ADD A ZERO TO THE PRICE AND ASK YOURSELF IF YOU WOULD STILL BUY IT, OR EVEN WANT IT!

#YOURBESTYOU
IF AN OUTFIT HAS BEEN HANGING IN YOUR WARDROBE UNDER PLASTIC FOR MORE THAN THREE YEARS, IT'S TIME TO LET IT GO!

your body shape. Often the honest appraisal of what you are is about accepting that you're never going to be Angelina Jolie and that what you've got isn't all that bad after all, once you know how to work it! But the first step has to be understanding who you are, and that means taking a look at your own lifestyle (again, unfortunately not Angelina Jolie's!).

We've devised a way for you to calculate easily how you apportion your time and, therefore, who you really are. Follow us into the illuminating world of the lifestyle pie chart. In the pie chart, you break down your lifestyle into chunks of time, i.e., how much of your week is spent in the following categories:

> WORK TIME — OBVIOUS, THIS ONE!
> PLAY TIME — SOCIAL ACTIVITIES, DINNER WITH YOUR PARTNER OR AN OUTING WITH FRIENDS.
> SHOW TIME — SPECIAL FUNCTIONS, LIKE WEDDINGS, CHRISTENINGS, ETC.
> DAY TIME — EVERYTHING FROM THE SCHOOL RUN TO LUNCH WITH THE GIRLS
> DOWN TIME — SUPERMARKET TO BANK, THIS IS THE CAMPAIGN TO DITCH THE FLEECE AND JEANS.

If we sleep eight hours a day, on average, we have 112 hours left every week in which to live our busy lives (we've done the maths so you don't have to!). Let's make this even easier and round that figure down to 100. Start by calculating the smallest piece of pie, Show Time, for life's big celebrations: weddings, significant birthdays, christenings, etc. How many would you attend every year? Four? Eight? Maybe ten in a very busy year? Assuming each event lasts eight hours, multiply the number of events by eight. That gives you 64hrs, which is a little more than 1 hour per week, or 1% of your pie chart, as your whole pie is 100%.

With work, it's a little easier as our schedules tend to average out over one week. So, if you work a 40-hour week, that's around 40% of your pie, and so on.

Here are two lifestyle pie charts for women with different lives. The first is for 'Mary', a woman who works part time:

Work time =   24hrs per week   24% of weekly activity

Play Time =   5hrs per week   5% of weekly activity

Day Time =   38hrs per week   38% of weekly activity

Show Time = 1hr per week!   1% of weekly activity

Down Time = 32hrs per week   32% of weekly activity

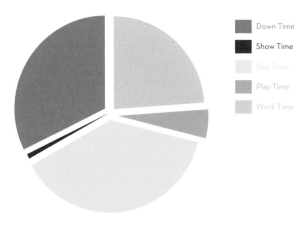

The second is a businesswoman and mother, who is required to attend evening functions as part of her job. Let's call her Sonya!

Work Time = 46hrs per week   46% of weekly activity

Play Time =   14hrs per week   14% of weekly activity

Day Time =   16hrs per week   16% of weekly activity

Show Time = 1 hr per week   1% of weekly activity

Down Time = 23hrs per week   23% of weekly activity

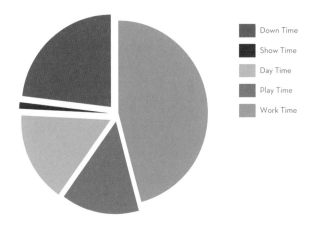

Now, fill in your own lifestyle pie chart, being as honest as possible. By the way, calculating your Down Time, i.e. your time to relax, is a really good way to see how you can apportion it more beneficially to you.

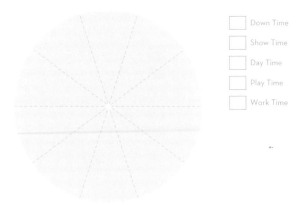

- [ ] Down Time
- [ ] Show Time
- [ ] Day Time
- [ ] Play Time
- [ ] Work Time

As you can see, there's a big difference in the wardrobe requirements of each woman. For example, Sonya will need to spend more on her work wardrobe and Mary on her Day Time dressing. Assessing your lifestyle needs can allow you to spend your budget wisely, most of the time, and allow for the odd moment of madness or flight of fancy.

So, if you spend most of your time at work, and don't wear a uniform, invest in your professional look. Don't fall into the trap of going into autopilot and becoming bored and lazy with your work persona. Not only will you feel much better about yourself but, as in today's world you are your own calling card, dress for the job you want — not the job you have.

If you spend most of your time in casual wear, we can help you find a way to feel good about how you look doing even the most boring of chores. It's actually one of the most commonly asked questions. Once the structure of formality is taken away most of us feel a bit sloppy in casual wear, but it doesn't have to be so!

We recently spoke to a group of professional women and asked them where they felt their difficulties lay in style terms. Was it getting dressed for work (Work Time), going out (Play Time), big occasions (Show Time), smart-casual (Day Time) or relaxing (Down Time). We discovered that the biggest difficulty for these intelligent, successful women was how to feel good in their Day

Time and Down Time modes — in other words, the problems begin when the armour comes off. We think that there's a new way to think about casual dressing that is as high on the feel-good factor and structure as on comfort and style.

Once you've cracked the pie chart, it's easy to see what lifestyle you're dressing. Now, all you have to do is decipher what body shape you're dressing. But first things first! Once you've had a look at your lifestyle pie chart, it's time to dig a little deeper, or look at the problem from a slightly different angle. What are your *daily*, *weekly* and *monthly* wardrobe requirements? This will help you to really get a sense of your needs.

You can ask yourself a few questions to begin with:

> WHAT KIND OF LIFE DO I LEAD, WHAT TYPE OF PERSON AM I?
> IS MY LIFE VERY BUSY? AM I QUITE ACTIVE? DO I MOSTLY DRIVE OR WALK? IS MY LIFE SEDENTARY?
> DO I NEED FREEDOM TO MOVE IN MY CLOTHING?
> DO I NEED TO LOOK PROFESSIONAL MOST OF THE TIME?
> DO I JUST WANT TO LOOK MORE STYLISH?
> AM I TRYING TO ATTRACT A PARTNER?
> HOW WOULD MY FRIENDS DESCRIBE ME AND MY STYLE?

I think we'd probably agree that many of us are a combination of the above: sometimes our lives are super busy with lots of professional and personal demands placed on us. Sometimes our lives are nice and quiet and we get time to chill and reflect, and sometimes we have a gaggle of children who completely take over our existence and no time to think at all! Whatever your life, in order to really nail your wardrobe requirements, i.e. what your clothes need to do for you, we need to look a little closer at the actual demands on you and your wardrobe.

Start by breaking down your day, then dissect your week, then have a closer look at your month and, finally, take a nice broad view of your year. What do you need from your wardrobe? It's a slightly different way of looking at things to your lifestyle pie chart, but should throw up some interesting results!

DEBBIE COLE, MULLINGAR

'I THINK BEAUTY IS WOMEN WITH CURVES, WHO DON'T TRY TO HIDE THEIR AGE, EMBRACING THEIR WOMANHOOD AND ENJOYING IT. I THINK I AM BEAUTIFUL BECAUSE I AM HAPPY WITH WHO I AM: I HAVE FOUR CHILDREN, I AM IN MY 40S AND THERE IS A SELF-CONFIDENCE THAT COMES FROM THAT, THAT YOU DON'T HAVE IN YOUNGER YEARS.'

YOUR DAY

Could consist of a school run, grocery shopping, lunch with a friend, chores, a part-time job, preparing dinner, and meeting friends.

Or, it could be . . . work all day, then meet friends.

Or, it could be . . . school run, drop baby to crèche, work full time, take meetings, meet friend. What's the picture of your day looking like? Do you need more work wear than casual, more practical hardwearing clothes for your active life?

YOUR WEEK

Now, start to look at the broader picture: recurring pastimes, wardrobe expectations slightly outside your daily norms: your evening class, the gym. What are your weekends like? If you don't need work wear, what kind of casuals do you need?

YOUR MONTH

Now include events, birthday parties, launches, parent-teacher meetings.

YOUR YEAR

Here, you factor in Christmas, weddings and all other annual events for which you'll need formal or smart wear.

When you have had a look at the key activities of your life, you can start to piece together a picture of your fundamental wardrobe requirements.

Let's make up an example for the purpose of illustration:

Aileen is 32 and has two small children. She is married to Jack. They live in Meath and both work full time in an office in Dublin. Aileen needs to look professional but also likes to try and catch up with friends whenever she can. They have an active social and personal life. Aileen is going to need a wardrobe that will enable her to:

> GET READY QUICKLY AND EASILY
> LOOK PROFESSIONAL (SHE ALSO WANTS TO LOOK GOOD)
> GO FROM WORK TO PLAY EASILY
> GO SHOPPING AND CHASE KIDS
> ENJOY HER WEEKENDS AND HAVE GOING-OUT CLOTHES FOR MEETING FRIENDS

Just reading over this example, you can see lots of opportunities for cross-over from work to play to down time. Have a go, what are the key activities of your week and what do you want your clothes to say about you? Welcome to your weekly planner! This is the perfect way for you to plot your average week in terms of clothing and style. The first planner is for you to note your style choices over an average week. Try and pick a week that contains a representative spread of your usual activities. This will really make you think about your approach to getting dressed, and awareness is the first step. What's important to establish is not only what you wore, but also how it made you feel.

The second planner is for when you've graduated from the school of *Your Best You*. Revisit the process when your confidence is higher and your knowledge about who you are and what you are is at full speed. Again, charting how your new wardrobe choices make you feel is an important indicator of what we all already knew: looking good makes us feel good.

MY WEEKLY PLANNER — BEFORE

	WHAT I WAS DOING	WHAT I WORE	HOW I FELT
MONDAY			
MORNING			
AFTERNOON			
EVENING			
TUESDAY			
MORNING			
AFTERNOON			
EVENING			
WEDNESDAY			
MORNING			
AFTERNOON			
EVENING			
THURSDAY			
MORNING			
AFTERNOON			
EVENING			
FRIDAY			
MORNING			
AFTERNOON			
EVENING			
SATURDAY			
MORNING			
AFTERNOON			
EVENING			
SUNDAY			
MORNING			
AFTERNOON			
EVENING			

MY WEEKLY PLANNER — AFTER

	WHAT I WAS DOING	WHAT I WORE	HOW I FELT
MONDAY			
MORNING			
AFTERNOON			
EVENING			
TUESDAY			
MORNING			
AFTERNOON			
EVENING			
WEDNESDAY			
MORNING			
AFTERNOON			
EVENING			
THURSDAY			
MORNING			
AFTERNOON			
EVENING			
FRIDAY			
MORNING			
AFTERNOON			
EVENING			
SATURDAY			
MORNING			
AFTERNOON			
EVENING			
SUNDAY			
MORNING			
AFTERNOON			
EVENING			

#YOURBESTYOU

MANY WOMEN RESIST CHANGE BECAUSE THEY ARE UNHAPPY WITH THEIR DRESS SIZE. DON'T WAIT FOR THE WEIGHT TO GO! DEVELOP YOUR STYLE AND BE YOUR BEST YOU BASED ON WHO YOU ARE *TODAY.*

HOW DO YOU WANT TO LOOK?

Now that you've taken a detailed look at your lifestyle, it's time to look at who you'd like to be. At first glance this seems like an obvious, maybe even silly question: how do you want to look? But it's a useful question, because most of us have a natural tendency to focus on the negative. Often, when we first speak to women they can tell us exactly what they hate about themselves and how they DON'T want to look (which is often how they look right now!) but when asked the very pertinent and appropriate question, 'How do you want to look?', they are very often stumped! Women who spend the vast majority of their time loathing how they look forget to think about how they would like to look. Just starting here and addressing what you *do* want can be very beneficial to the overall process of change and development.

Start to think about how you want to look, what impression you would like to give, what you would like your clothes to say about you: that you're a smart and sassy businesswoman, a capable mum, a reliable friend? The fact of the matter is that we judge people by their appearance; in fact, we make our minds up about a person within the first 15 seconds of meeting them, so how you look determines how people perceive you. But more than that, how you look directly affects how you feel about yourself and, ultimately, how confidently you present yourself to the outside world.

If you think you look good, you feel good. If you think you look great, you feel great.

SALLY FAWCETT-WHITE, DUBLIN

'I AM CONFIDENT AND COMFORTABLE WITH WHO I AM AND THAT'S WHAT MAKES ME BEAUTIFUL! REAL BEAUTY IS HAVING CONFIDENCE, KINDNESS, AND AN AWARENESS OF PEOPLE AND THE ENVIRONMENT AROUND YOU.'

IF YOU HAD A MAGIC WAND

WHAT WOULD YOU MAKE YOUR WARDROBE DO FOR YOU?

First, lets take a closer look at the problem, Madam . . . Using the page opposite as a workbook, make a list of what you hate about your wardrobe, and then make a list of what you *want*: what are your dream pieces, and how do they fit with your lifestyle? Here are a few common wardrobe misdemeanours to get you started, but remember, let's be as honest but as positive as possible. It's never as bad as you think!

THE LOOK TRAP

Do you constantly wear the same clothes — are you in a sartorial cul de sac? Write a list of the offending garments: that pair of jeans you've worn for five years, the bobbly jumper you can't live without, the jacket that doesn't really fit . . .

THE BLACK TRAP

Do you think black makes you look slimmer and therefore live in the colour? So much so, you can't see any light at the end of the tunnel?

FLEECE FETISHIST

You find snuggly comfort in your big soft fleeces but also believe they hide your body. You wear them so often you look like a multicoloured sheep . . .

#YOURBESTYOU

IF BLACK MAKES UP MORE THAN 60% OF YOUR WARDROBE, YOU ARE IN THE BLACK TRAP! SHIFT THE BALANCE TO GREY, NAVY OR BROWN TO FREE YOURSELF.

AVERSION TO COLOUR

Does colour make you cringe? Allergic to apple green? Blue about wearing blue?

CAMOUFLAGE

Here, list your armoury of camouflage wear — what garments do you hide behind? Be honest, list your barricades, those over-sized, baggy clothes that are comfy but that you know add inches.

MY WARDROBE LIKES/DISLIKES

LIKES

DISLIKES

WHAT ARE YOUR DREAM PIECES?

Really think outside the box here. What would you love in your wardrobe? Here are some suggested headings to get you going. If you're short on ideas, check in the capsule wardrobe list in chapter 4.

› THE PERFECT DRESS
› THE KILLER PENCIL SKIRT
› THE BEST POSSIBLE JEANS
› A SKIRT FOR ALL SEASONS
› YOUR BEST TOPS
› TROUSERS THAT LOVE YOUR BODY
› A REALLY SMART JACKET/COAT
› KILLER HEELS THAT DON'T KILL YOUR FEET!

FIND YOUR INSPIRATION
BECOME FAMILIAR WITH THE LANGUAGE OF STYLE

This is the fun part! Never has so much inspiration been so readily available to so many of us and in so many forms. There are a million magazines, websites, reference books, celebrities, TV shows and films that can inspire. The key is figuring out the best way for you to tap in to material or put simply, 'stuff you like', that inspires you.

How can you use inspiration to your advantage? For us, the best examples come from the world of fashion, because in fashion, designers are constantly looking for inspiration. They are charged with developing and designing a new collection twice a year, spring and autumn, and now, with the advent of 'resort' collections, designers have to come up with four collections a year and some are responsible for more than one label. With that in mind, they are constantly looking for new ideas to inspire designs that people will want to buy. In fact, designers will often say that finding new ideas and new inspiration is the most difficult part of the creative process . . . and yet it's essential. When we give advice, we look not just at our girl and her lifestyle and body shape, her taste and personal style boundaries, but also, we look to movies, music, design, celebrity, to add that extra something. That *joie de vivre*!

So, how can you learn to tap into your creative flow?

First, more than clothes, broaden your horizons. Anything can inspire you and us, it could be the shape of a shampoo bottle or the colour of a car. It could be a kooky old lady on the street or movie star, like Meryl Streep. Inspiration is everywhere; all you have to do is see it. Look at your favourite films, immerse yourself in magazines, go online, just start to OPEN YOUR EYES. Enjoy images and ask yourself why you like them.

Finding your inspiration opens your mind to new possibilities with your image, which means that you can now look at clothes

#YOURBESTYOU

SO YOU'VE STARTED TO LOOK AT THE WORLD SLIGHTLY DIFFERENTLY NOW. READ MORE MAGAZINES AND LOOK AT IMAGES NOT JUST FOR GOSSIP (WHICH IS OK!) BUT ALSO FOR IDEAS AND INSPIRATION.

to which you would normally never give the time of day. Then, you can go a step further and try on clothes you would *never* normally try on.

We make our fabulous makeover girls do that all the time. We need to open their minds pretty quickly, so we just jump straight in there and get them trying on a ton of clothes they would normally quite happily walk past. This is often the toughest point of the makeover and the one where we traditionally meet the most resistance (there have been plenty of tears at this juncture!). Our girls can feel very vulnerable, but this part of the process is imperative in order to:

1. GET THEM THINKING ABOUT THEMSELVES IN A NEW LIGHT
2. FIND INSPIRATIONS TO CREATE THEIR NEW WARDROBE
3. SEE THE BIGGER PICTURE

We promise you, by the end of the day, if you stick with it, you will feel exhilarated and excited by the process of pushing yourself out of your comfort zone and trying new ideas.

SEEING THE BIGGER PICTURE

It is worth mentioning here that as you start to apply our simple tips and advice, you will start to see the bigger picture. On a very simplistic and real level, you'll be spending more time in a full-length mirror and this little action alone will help you to start to see your entire silhouette and not just the bits you hate. You'll start to see that it's not really as bad as you thought. That the negative thinking, outlook and view you have built of yourself over time can be changed. This negative approach needs to be corroded away, and it takes a little work and effort on your part. But stick with it, because the results will be amazing.

One practical way of putting this new open-mindedness and grasp of beauty to its best use is to find a *realistic style role model.* Pick a person whose style you love. Sounds simple, but think long and hard about this — and here's the really important bit — pick someone who has a similar body shape to you. So, now this style inspiration will also be practical. There is someone for everyone! Think of this person as your personal style guide. They don't have to be a celebrity, although it does help if you pick someone whose changing style you get to see regularly. It doesn't have to be Kim Kardashian or even Kate Middleton; it could be your mum or your sister or your very sexy and glamorous aunt.

DRESS FOR SUCCESS DUBLIN
SONYA'S NEWEST BABY!

Recently, I opened the first Irish office of global not-for-profit organisation Dress for Success in Dublin (www.dressforsuccessdublin.org). It's been hard work putting everything in place, building a charity from scratch, the network and the bank balance, but it's been worthwhile. So what is Dress for Success?

'The mission of Dress for Success is to promote the economic independence of women in need by providing professional attire, a network of support and the career-development tools to help women thrive in work and in life.

'Dress for Success gives free consultations and free suiting to women who are in need, to help them to gain financial independence. Over 600,000 women have been dressed by Dress for Success worldwide, helping them to secure their futures.

'And why do we do this? Because we know that if you are not looking your best, you can't do your best, and because we only get one chance to make a first impression. We also know that the confidence of a mother greatly affects the confidence of the children.'

Could there be a more powerful charter for feeling good about yourself? Get the balance right and what you achieve is control over one more portion of your life.

And the brilliant thing is, you can have as many as you like. We recommend picking three to start with, as it helps to keep the mind focused on what you are trying to achieve. Make Google Images your best friend.

FAMOUS STYLE GUIDES

› VICTORIA BECKHAM CITES HER PERSONAL STYLE GUIDE AS AUDREY HEPBURN

› SONYA'S PERSONAL STYLE GUIDE IS SONIA RYKIEL

› BRENDAN'S PERSONAL STYLE GUIDE IS MENSWEAR DESIGNER THOM BROWNE

MOOD BOARDS AND SCRAPBOOKS

For day-to-day inspiration, keep a scrapbook, slot tears ('tears' are literally pictures you tear from magazines) into it and keep notes. This will build up over time and is always lovely to have to hand to recap and look over what caught your attention. This is a very sweet and personal insight into your taste and what you like, in terms of colour shape and form. There are some great websites that also allow you to build up scrapbooks of things you find: **www.tumblr.com**, pinterest (**www.pinterest.com**) and Instagram (**www.instagram.com**) are three we love.

You will probably have a friend who created a mood board for her wedding dress or even wedding (maybe it was you). With a mood board, you can focus all your attention onto one space or board. This way you get an overall picture of your evolving taste. Go through magazines and find images of pieces you like and start to build your very own board for your style and personality. It will really help inspire, build confidence and direct your tastes. Plus, it's fun!

So now you're laden with new-found insights about yourself and your wardrobe needs. You've gone to the trouble of finding out who you are and who you want to be, and you might be asking yourself why? I know I'm not happy with how I look, but if I crack the code of lifestyle and body shape, what difference will it make? Well, you only have to read the case histories of our makeover candidates to know that successfully completing the process can lead to a massive shift in your confidence and self-esteem. Now you know who you are and what you want. Let's do it!

#YOURBESTYOU

MAKE YOUR RESEARCH VISIBLE — HANG YOUR MOOD BOARD SOMEWHERE YOU'LL SEE IT EVERY DAY: IN YOUR WARDROBE OR IN THE KITCHEN, IT'S UP TO YOU!

WHAT SHAPE ARE YOU TODAY?

CHAPTER 2

BODY SHAPE IS OF HUGE SOCIAL AND CULTURAL IMPORTANCE. IN BRAZIL, THE COUNTRY PERCEIVED TO HAVE THE HIGHEST PERCENTAGE OF 'PERFECT BODIES' (AND THE HIGHEST INCIDENCE OF PLASTIC SURGERY TOO!) THERE'S A TAKE-NO-PRISONERS ATTITUDE. BETWEEN THE BEACH AND CARNIVAL, YOU'RE GOING TO BE TAKING YOUR CLOTHES OFF IN FRONT OF YOUR GREATER COMMUNITY AT SOME STAGE, SO PLAY THE GAME OR STAY AT HOME!

IN FRANCE, A WOMAN is reportedly given three months to spring back to her pre-pregnancy body or else; it's easy to see why thinness is culturally embedded in that country.

In Italy, the story goes that a young girl has a tiny hole in the palm side of her ring finger, through which everything she eats passes. Once she is married, the hole is blocked by the wedding ring and all that pasta takes its toll. So, the message is, until you get your man it's La Dolce Vita, but afterwards, well, we know what happens.

It's clear from these examples that women the world over are subjected to rigid rules about their body shape. But what's the connection between body shape and body image? Well, they are actually two very different things, divided by the towering might of confidence. Those who lack it are prone to negative body image and those who have it are predisposed to a positive body image, regardless of size or shape.

Many of us are in some form of denial or delusion about our true body shape. Denial involves not recognising our true body shape, thinking you're a size 16 when you're actually a size 20, or a size 8 when you're actually a 4. Delusion acknowledges dissatisfaction with body shape but magnifies it. 'My hips are huge, I'm a size 16' often ends up being diagnosed as a size 12 hourglass shape who hasn't realised that it's not her hips that are big, but her waist that's small, and just doesn't understand how to dress for her shape — but more of this later.

The fact is, so many of us aren't happy with what we've got. We've often spoken in front of a large audience and asked the question, 'Hands up if you are a hundred per cent happy with how you look?' In a room that size, you might get one or two hands in the air. At best that's 0.66% of us who are completely happy with how we look. Not a very cheery tale is it?

So, why are we so dissatisfied? There are lots of reasons. We are bombarded with images of 'perfection' beaming out at us from the covers of magazines, TV programmes and films. The newsflash is that those people pay others to make them look that good: their image is their career and paying for a personal trainer or stylist is an investment worth making.

But there's more to it than that. The seeds of our body image are sown long before we choose the actress or model we most want to look like. A recent study of girls as young as six in the UK revealed that over 60% believed that they needed to lose weight. The children were shown seven pictures of themselves, the middle one being their actual body size with the three on either side manipulated to show them increasingly thin and increasingly fat. Most of the girls believed themselves to be larger than they actually were and most chose a slimmer version of themselves as their ideal body shape.

This is very worrying. Given that attitudinal references at that age predominantly come from the home, could we be passing on our own foibles to our children? Perhaps we do this unconsciously, (or even consciously) verbalising our own negative feelings about our bodies. Think of it: 'Ah, poor Grainne has my hips/bum/tum.' (Delete where appropriate!) In other words, it's my baggage and I will off-load it onto you as your birthright! Grainne, your hips/bum/tum are grand — as are your mum's.

We have a duty to focus on the positive for the sake of future generations. Don't focus on what's bad about your physical inheritance, but on what you can be proud of. Don't focus on what you can't eat, but on all the wonderful healthy foods that you can enjoy together. We can enjoy promoting a positive body image and seeing our daughters grow up into happy, confident women who are proud of their bodies.

SO, WHAT IS BODY IMAGE?
ACCORDING TO EATINGDISORDERS.IE

- Body image is multifaceted and refers to the individual's perceptions of, and attitudes towards the body, especially its appearance.

- It is a complex set of ideas, judgements, attitudes, and feelings of 'the self', which gives a picture of one in one's mind's eye, and a sense of the space we occupy. It also includes ideas about how others view us!

- Body image is said to be elastic, which means it is changeable through the presentation of new information.

- It is said that people have a body-esteem schema, which dominates functioning.

- We all have subjective opinions of how we look — how old or young, fat or thin, tall or small, beautiful or ugly we are.

- Our inner body image is central to how we feel about ourselves; as such a major part of self-esteem is connected with how we feel we look — hence the connection between body image and self-image.

- Body image is a core part of our personality and affects life in many ways, especially in the case of people with eating disorders, whose self-evaluation is unduly influenced by the value they place on shape and weight. This value placed on shape and weight then affects self-image/esteem.

- People with poor self-esteem could feel relaxed about their appearance, however with people with a poor body image, it is unlikely they could feel good about themselves.

- The connection between self-image and weight is particularly strong in women, due to cultural pressure and high levels of social comparison. Also, we overestimate our body size and shape consistently!

> *POOR BODY IMAGE INFLUENCES INCLUDE:*
>
> *• Past experiences*
>
> *• Body weight and timing of puberty*
>
> *• Teasing/bullying*
>
> *• Exposure to parental weight concerns*
>
> *• Abuse or assault*
>
> *• Negative attitudes in early adolescence*
>
> *• Present experiences*
>
> *• Feedback from others*
>
> *• Abnormal attention due to distinctive physical features*
>
> *• Media*
>
> *• Self-image*
>
> *• Flawed Values*
>
> *• Overestimation of size*

So, how we see ourselves may often not be connected to our actual shape. But what's so important about shape anyway? Well, it's clear that it's an emotive issue. Every international fashion week provokes some media uproar about 'skinny models' or, recently, the use of 'curvy models' — imagine that? We've both been present backstage at international fashion shows, and yes, the girls are very thin, some unbearably so, but clothes drape and flow beautifully on them. However, fashion is fantasy and real life is for real people to live. Remember,

> THIN AND ATTRACTIVE ARE NOT NECESSARILY THE SAME THING
> SOPHIA LOREN IS SEXIER THAN AUDREY HEPBURN
> MEN LIKE CURVES

Very often people see what you tell them to see. That is the allure of the confident woman: she believes in herself, giving everyone else no option but to believe the message. The most attractive thing a woman can wear is a smile: it is the shorthand for happy and confident, and this works at any age and any size. But it's very hard to wear a smile if you're draped in tent-like camouflage to hide the bits of your body that you hate.

So, understanding body shape is a passport to making the most of your assets while understanding how to gently conceal the bits of yourself that you're not so keen on, but how can we work out our body shape?

For about ten years now, television shows, magazines and pundits have been preaching to women about 'body shape'. The remarkable thing is that, despite all this talking and blanket coverage, most of us don't understand what shape we are, or, more importantly, why it matters. You would not believe how many times women will run up to us on the street, unceremoniously fling open their outerwear and ask, 'What shape am I?' At a glance, we can give them the answer: very often not the one they expected. However, that's not the end of the story: knowing your body shape is one thing, understanding how to apply that information to your wardrobe is quite another.

LET'S DIAGNOSE

For us, diagnosing body shape can't be separated from a framework for dressing that shape to create balance and ultimately confidence by making the most of what you've got. To make things simple, we've pared it right back to the four most commonly occurring shapes:

› PEAR

› APPLE

› HOURGLASS

› RULER

Using one of our four gorgeous makeover women to illustrate each body shape.

AUDREY GREENE, WICKLOW

'BEAUTY ISN'T ALWAYS ABOUT THE LOOK, IT IS ABOUT THE REAL PERSON. IT HAS TAKEN ME A LONG TIME TO ACCEPT HOW I LOOK AND I KNOW I WILL NEVER BE A HUNDRED PER CENT HAPPY WITH MY LOOKS, BUT MY INNER BEAUTY IS REALLY WHAT MAKES ME, ME.'

GABRIELLE DAVY, DUBLIN

'REAL BEAUTY IS KNOWING WHO YOU ARE AND WHAT YOUR BEST POINTS ARE AND CELEBRATING THAT IN YOUR STYLE AND DAY-TO-DAY LIFE. I'VE GOT THE CLASSIC IRISH LOOKS — RED HAIR AND FRECKLES. IN EVERY OTHER COUNTRY IN THE WORLD, I'M CONSIDERED EXOTIC.'

HOW TO DIAGNOSE YOUR BODY SHAPE

So here goes, girls! Let's do it! We have developed a very simple equation using Pythagoras' theorem (kidding) — but we *are* using triangles to help us and you to very simply and clearly diagnose and identify your body shape. In our last book and in the past we traditionally used six body shapes as our guides. Pear, Apple, Hourglass, Petite, Amazonian and Ruler. While these were brilliant templates for you, we have figured out an even simpler way to diagnose body shape, using one simple question and four shapes.

Firstly, ask yourself, 'Waist or no waist?'

Do you think you have a naturally occurring curved waist or not? Importantly, this has nothing to do with dress size. Stand in front of the mirror and determine whether your natural waist curves in or out. Now, using that information, get a tape measure if possible, or a piece of string will do, or even a belt, and take two measurements to determine your *hip-to-shoulder ratio.* That is, the distance between your hips and then the distance between your shoulders. Which measurement is wider, your hips or your shoulders? Or are they the same width apart?

If your hips are wider than your shoulders, you are a Pear. If your shoulders are wider than your hips, you are an Apple. If your hips and shoulders are equidistant, you are either an Hourglass or a Ruler, which one you are is determined by the waist measurement.

PEAR

In simple terms, you are a very subtle triangle shape. Pears tend to have flat tummies. You have lots of positives, like a lovely slender upper body, great arms and that typical tiny waist. Your problem areas are your hips, thighs and bum.

APPLE

In simple terms, you are an upside-down triangle. Apples have great legs. Your problem area is your mid-section, which is where you hold all your weight. You have lovely slender limbs, and normally a great décolletage. Your narrowest point is at the top of your rib cage.

HOURGLASS

In simple terms, your hips and shoulders are the same width apart, creating the graphic shape of two triangles tip to tip. You are the ultimate shape. You could be size 8 or 28 and still be an hourglass.

RULER

Again, your hips and shoulders are the same width apart, but you have to work to define your waist. You have model-like proportions, though: wonderful, slender legs and great hips and bum.

REMEMBER: THERE IS NO RIGHT OR WRONG SIZE.

Now that you've measured yourself to determine what shape you are, you can pick and choose from the advice and information we provide in the following chapters and combine the various sartorial guides to style your best you. But first, let's take a look at our four gorgeous makeover women, who illustrate perfectly each body shape.

LOUISE MCSHERRY IS OUR
PEACHY PEAR

LOUISE, FROM CLONSILLA, DUBLIN, WORKS FULL TIME AS AN ACCOUNTANT, AND IS MUM TO FABULOUS TWO-YEAR-OLD DAUGHTER, ELLIE.

LOUISE SAYS, 'I PARTICIPATE IN A LOT OF SPORTS LIKE CAMOGIE AND RUNNING AND SO THE PART OF MY BODY I HATE THE MOST IS MY THIGHS. I REALLY DISLIKE HOW CHUNKY THEY ARE. I ALSO DON'T LIKE MY BUM. IT'S TOO BIG!

'AS MY TOP AND BOTTOM PARTS ARE BOTH DIFFERENT SIZES, IT'S HARD TO FIND SOMETHING THAT FITS RIGHT. MOST STUFF IS EITHER TOO BIG ON THE TOP AND THEN TOO TIGHT ON THE BOTTOM, OR VICE VERSA. I FIND IT HARD LOOKING AT THINGS LIKE TROUSERS AND SKINNY JEANS, KNOWING THAT I COULDN'T POSSIBLY WEAR THEM WITH MY FIGURE. I STILL DON'T FEEL LIKE I DRESS MY AGE. DURING THE DAY [WHEN NOT WORKING] I AM ALWAYS IN TRAKKIE BOTTOMS OR JEANS, AS I FIND THEM SO COMFORTABLE. I FIND IT HARD TO FIND CASUAL CLOTHES THAT ARE AS COMFORTABLE OR FIT ME AS WELL AS JEANS DO.'

1 MEASURE THE DISTANCE BETWEEN YOUR SHOULDERS

2 MEASURE THE DISTANCE BETWEEN YOUR HIPS

3 IF YOUR HIPS ARE WIDER THAN YOUR SHOULDERS YOU ARE A PEAR

PEAR =

AOIFE RYAN IS OUR
FABULOUS
RULER

AOIFE IS A FULL-TIME STUDENT AND PART-TIME MODEL (LOTS OF RULERS ARE!).

AOIFE SAYS, 'I SOMETIMES HATE HAVING SMALL BOOBS, BECAUSE I CAN'T WEAR CERTAIN DRESSES. I HATE HAVING FRECKLES SOMETIMES (EVEN THOUGH PEOPLE ALWAYS SAY THEY LOVE MY FRECKLES).

'BECAUSE I'M QUITE TALL (5'10") AND HAVE A SMALL WAIST/HIPS, IT'S SOMETIMES HARD TO FIND CERTAIN CLOTHES, SUCH AS JEANS, THAT FIT ME IN THE RIGHT PLACES.

'I NEVER CHOOSE THINGS THAT GO WELL WITH MY BODY SHAPE OR WHAT SUITS ME; I SOMETIMES BUY SOMETHING THAT EVERYONE IS WEARING AND THEN REALISE AFTER WEARING IT A COUPLE OF TIMES, IT ACTUALLY DOES NOTHING FOR ME. I'M ALSO VERY BAD AT INTRODUCING SOME COLOUR INTO MY WARDROBE, BECAUSE I HAVE IT IN MY HEAD TO BE SAFE WHEN WEARING CLOTHES AND THEREFORE ALWAYS GO FOR BLACKS, GREYS, BROWNS, ETC.'

AS THE NAME SUGGESTS, RULERS' BIG ISSUE IS THE LACK OF CURVES. THEY TEND TO HAVE SLIM HIPS, SHOULDERS AND THEREFORE NO WAIST.

RULER =

MARY GRAHAM IS OUR
LUSCIOUS APPLE

FROM PALMERSTOWN IN DUBLIN, MARY IS A WORKING MUM AND HAS FOUR WONDERFUL CHILDREN AGED 15-27.

MARY SAYS, 'THE THING I HATE MOST ABOUT SHOPPING IS MY ABILITY TO CHOOSE THE MOST UNFLATTERING OUTFITS FOR MYSELF. I NEVER GET IT RIGHT.

'I ALSO HATE, HATE, HATE THE DIFFERENCE IN SIZE, DEPENDING ON WHICH STORE YOU ARE IN. AS FOR MY BODY ISSUES . . . I HATE MY REALLY BIG, SPARE, ROTUND BELLY, MY ARMS THAT LOOK LIKE LEGS AND THE WAY MY BREASTS SPILL OUT OVER THE SIDE OF MY BRA.

'ALL ROUND, I HAVE TO SAY IT'S BEEN A LONG TIME SINCE I'VE BEEN ON A SHOPPING TRIP FOR MYSELF THAT I'VE ENJOYED. MY DAUGHTER LAURA SAYS, "SUCK IT UP — IT'S HARD WORK BEING FABULOUS!" WE KEEP ON TRYING IN THE HOPE THAT ONE DAY I WILL BE THE, "LITTLE LESS THAN FABULOUS" *OLD* ME THAT I WOULD LOVE TO BE.'

AFTER OUR DAY, MARY SAID, 'I'VE STARTED ON A NEW BEAUTY REGIME AND AM LOOKING AFTER MY HEALTH. I PUT THIS DOWN TO THE HELP AND ENCOURAGEMENT I GOT FROM ALL OF YOU ON MY VERY SPECIAL DAY.'

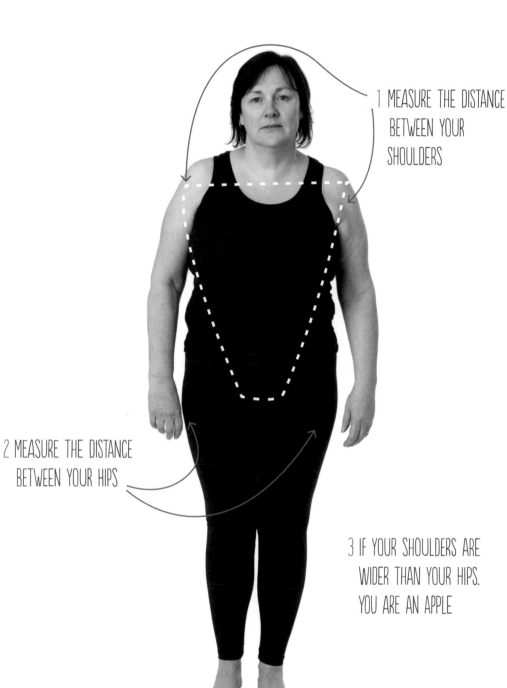

1 MEASURE THE DISTANCE BETWEEN YOUR SHOULDERS

2 MEASURE THE DISTANCE BETWEEN YOUR HIPS

3 IF YOUR SHOULDERS ARE WIDER THAN YOUR HIPS, YOU ARE AN APPLE

APPLE =

WENDY LOUISE KNIGHT
IS OUR
HOTTIE HOURGLASS

WENDY IS A VERY TALENTED MILLINER LIVING IN LONGFORD WITH HER FIVE LOVELY CHILDREN, AGED 4-14.

WENDY SAYS, 'I HATE MY TUMMY AND MY CHILDBEARING HIPS . . . I FIND IT HARD TO GET TROUSERS TO FIT, AS I HAVE A SMALL WAIST AND JUST DON'T FEEL COMFY IN FITTED CLOTHES. I AM REALLY BUSY AND JUST DON'T DO HEELS, SO IT TENDS TO BE SMOCK TOPS, BOOTS, LEGGINGS — SO WRONG!

'WHEN I DO BUY A SKIRT, IT NEVER FITS AND DRESSES SEEM ODD LENGTHS AS I HAVE LONG LEGS . . . SO I TEND TO GO FOR A SAFE LINE.'

AFTER OUR DAY, WENDY SAID, 'MY DAY WITH YOU GUYS WAS FAB! THE BRA FITTING WAS AMAZING AND HAS MADE A WORLD OF DIFFERENCE, I CAN'T BELIEVE I WAS WEARING THE WRONG SIZE.'

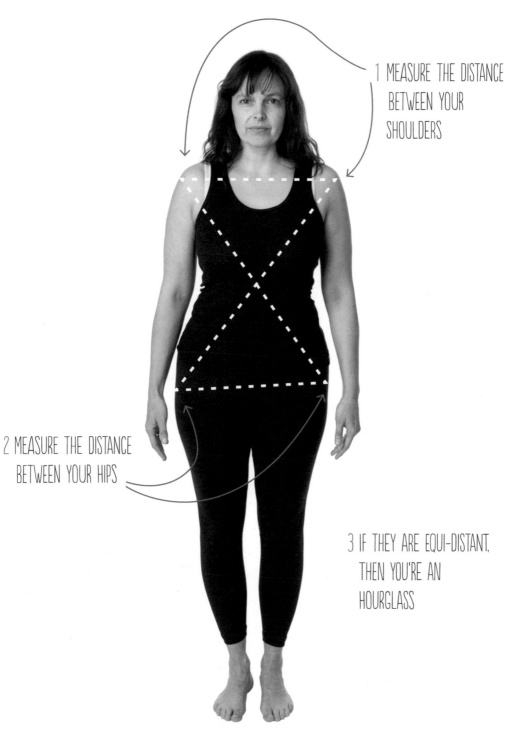

1 MEASURE THE DISTANCE BETWEEN YOUR SHOULDERS

2 MEASURE THE DISTANCE BETWEEN YOUR HIPS

3 IF THEY ARE EQUI-DISTANT, THEN YOU'RE AN HOURGLASS

HOURGLASS = ⧗

SHAPE VERSUS SIZE

Now that you've got your tape measures out and worked out what shape you are, you might well be wondering what this has to do with your size. It's clear to us that women have difficulties with size in clothes, as you can see from the following:

'SARAH', SIZE 16–20

'I hated having to rummage to the back of the rails to find my size, hidden away like a guilty secret. I felt that everyone was looking at me and feeling sorry for me, and more often than not, my size wasn't even there.'

'GEMMA', SIZE 4–6

'Shopping is really frustrating for me. It's practically impossible to find what I want to wear in my size. I can see the judgement on people's faces, some have even asked me if I'm anorexic to my face. It always ends the same way, with the suggestion that I try the children's department. I'm a 28-year-old woman – I don't want to wear children's clothes.'

Traditionally women have shopped by dress size. Well, the new mantra is 'shape not size'.

If you walk into the average clothes shop, the span of sizes is generally 8–18, that's six sizes. It's the Goldilocks effect – shops only catering to the women 'in the middle'. However, the real span of sizes in the adult female population goes from 4 (the equivalent of the famous American size zero) to 32 (stocked by Littlewoods and Simply Be). That's fifteen sizes, *nine* more sizes than stocked in the average shop. Now, we're sure that there are women smaller and bigger then those sizes, but we would be hard pushed to prescribe a shopping landscape for them.

Recent statistics show that the average size of an adult Irish woman is 14–16, with 40.5" hips. These statistics are evolving upwards and have been for centuries, long before fast food

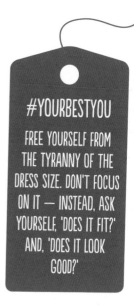

#YOURBESTYOU

FREE YOURSELF FROM THE TYRANNY OF THE DRESS SIZE. DON'T FOCUS ON IT — INSTEAD, ASK YOURSELF, 'DOES IT FIT?' AND, 'DOES IT LOOK GOOD?'

SARAH MOORE, KILKENNY

'BEAUTY COMES FROM THE INSIDE: WE MAY HAVE BIG TUMMIES OR CELLULITE ETC., BUT IT'S WHAT'S INSIDE THAT MATTERS. I'M BEAUTIFUL BECAUSE I'M A SINGLE MUM OF TWO FAB CHILDREN AND DO MY BEST IN LIFE EVERY SECOND OF THE DAY.'

could be blamed. Perhaps it would be more useful to gauge ourselves on the body mass index, or BMI, rather than judging ourselves with the tyranny of the unreliable dress size? Have you ever wondered why we obsess over handbags? They always fit. You can have an instant style hit without judgement; the same can be said of shoes.

The fact remains, however, that if you don't fall within the span of the golden six sizes (8–18) you have a problem. Your choice is immediately limited by the choices of others: the buyers in stores. It's hardly surprising that, bypassing high overheads and staff costs, the internet has become a fertile marketplace for the *niche* buyer.

Websites exist for pretty much anything you can imagine and fashion and style is no different. There are online stores for ladies with tiny feet and online stores for ladies with big feet, stores for below-average and above-average dress sizes. In our shopping guide, we go into detail on our top finds, but, for you the choice is probably pretty simple. You can either sit there complaining about what's not available to you, or embrace what is. The rights of the internet buyer are very secure in this country, and you are fully within your rights to return any items unused for a full refund if you contact the seller within ten days of receipt. You might incur postage costs, but that's a small price to pay to be able to buy with ease.

We are not suggesting that online shopping should take over from the hustle and bustle of our urban centres. On the contrary, we fervently support both independent retailers and global chains for their enrichment of our communities. And there are plenty of Goldilocks out there who will continue to shop within the narrow definitions set down by our traditional retailers through economic necessity. There are, however, bears of every shape and size out there that need their fashion fix.

The good news is that, looking forward, there is a very different landscape for the consumer. Recently, technology has spawned the emergence of 'crowd sourcing', which means we can all see the fashion collections six months before they hit the shops. Now, a consumer can pick from the catwalk what he or she will buy before it even goes into production, thereby fine-tuning the final offering by the designer. We are no longer being told what to buy, we are more accurately dictating to the providers.

Obviously, at the moment, only a tiny percentage of consumers fall into this bracket, at very high-end luxury prices. But actually, the effects are beginning to be felt for all, right down to the chainstores. Two seasons ago, Evans launched a range of clothing, which made sizing secondary to shape. The theory is, you can be pear, apple, or hourglass regardless of your dress size, but to look your best, getting the *shape* of your garment right for your body is more important than getting the *size* right.

So, after over ten years of prattling on about it, finally the results are there for the consumer. Body shape matters because understanding it helps us to make the right choices for our wardrobes and ourselves, and finally everyone, from high fashion to high street, understands that the consumer has the power.

UNDER-STANDING UNDER-WEAR

SO, NOW YOU'RE ARMED WITH ALL THE INFORMATION YOU NEED TO BEGIN TO CHANGE YOUR LOOK, ACCORDING TO YOUR LIFESTYLE AND BODY SHAPE. BUT BEFORE YOU JUMP INTO BUYING CLOTHES, IT'S IMPORTANT TO GET TO GRIPS WITH THE BASICS.

WHAT WE WEAR *under* our clothes has a huge impact on how we look. There are two very distinct roles that we need our underwear to fulfil: form and function. Firstly, function. Below, we will discuss the importance of a properly fitting bra, and anyone who has been paying any attention to us will know how evangelical we are about that. But that's only half the picture. How we cover our lower half is also a major issue. It seems like generations ago that the issue of VPL was introduced. Since then, the 'knicker' has evolved into a serious piece of kit, spanning in form anything from a micro-thong to all-encompassing body armour. Knowing what to choose is a path fraught with difficult decisions and often wasted money.

The aim of wearing foundation garments is to achieve a streamlined silhouette with the bust line in the right place.

A QUESTION OF FORM

There's nothing sexy going on in the above paragraph, is there? And we thought underwear was supposed to make us feel womanly and alluring. Well, it can when it's *lingerie*. Staring out at us from magazines and films is the classic image of the siren in matching lacy racing gear, and while we may not always have bodies to match, beautiful lingerie can make us feel that little bit more sensual and attractive. The good news is that lingerie works best on soft curves. A little inch of lace from your bra, peeking out from your dress, can look beautiful; being able to see the point at which your magic knickers lose control of your body does not. For your lingerie to be seen is ok; your underwear being seen is not!

So are underwear and lingerie mutually exclusive? They definitely used to be, but thanks to advances in fabrication and production and increased expectations from the consumer, in many instances the two have now married. It's no longer necessary to swathe yourself in industrial prosthetic-coloured casings to get a good silhouette. Women want to feel good in their skins, and the right foundations can go a long way to helping.

#YOURBESTYOU

THE BOOBS SHOULD BE EXACTLY HALF-WAY BETWEEN THE SHOULDERS AND THE ELBOWS. ❑

(TICK THIS BOX IF YOU JUST CHECKED.)

WHAT CAN THE RIGHT UNDERWEAR SOLUTIONS DO FOR YOU?

The offering in support underwear has grown over the past ten years to include waist-cinchers, bum-lifters and cellulite-diminishers. Some of them are well designed and effective; some are uncomfortable and downright unwearable, and all are pandering to women's all-consuming desire to be, or look, thinner, so *caveat emptor* is the order of the day. If your best friend/sister tells you that she's found the magic knickers to beat all magic knickers, naturally your urge is to rush out and buy salvation. Stop! This armour costs a pretty penny, so think about what it is you're trying to achieve. The first thing to do is assess your 'problem area': once you know the goal, you can choose appropriately. There's no point buying a garment that wrangles your thighs if it's your tummy that's the problem.

#YOURBESTYOU

WHEN CHOOSING SUPPORT WEAR, WORK BACKWARDS FROM WHAT YOU WILL BE WEARING TO ENSURE A STREAMLINED SILHOUETTE.

WHAT SUPPORT DO WE NEED?

Generally, the support falls into two camps, either bum, hips and thighs *or* tummy. There is, of course, the cover-all-bases option, the heavy artillery of support, which can either take the form of a wrestler suit or a slip. Increasingly, we are moving towards a slip as the support of choice. Think about when we use support wear: usually it's for that big occasion — a wedding, ball or party. What do women normally wear on these occasions? Our guess is that it's a dress in some form. Why tie yourself up in knots with magic knickers, open gussets and spillage when a slip can offer the streamlining that we're craving?

To simplify, we've broken down the offering into three categories, and paired them with the body shapes they work for.

LOWER-HALF SUPPORT PEAR, HOURGLASS

KNICKERS

HALF SLIP

MID-SECTION SUPPORT APPLE, RULER, HOURGLASS

WAIST-CINCHERS

CORSETRY

FULL BODY ARMOUR ALL BODY SHAPES

WRESTLER SUIT

FULL SLIP

IMELDA
MATCHETT,
CORK CITY

'REAL BEAUTY
COMES FROM
WITHIN AND
WHEN YOU ARE
COMPLETELY
COMFORTABLE
WITHIN YOURSELF,
YOUR BEAUTY
SHINES THROUGH.
I'M FINALLY AT
A POINT IN MY
LIFE WHERE I
AM ENTIRELY
COMFORTABLE
WITHIN MYSELF!
BEAUTY IS ONLY
IMAGE DEEP, BEING
COMFORTABLE IN
OUR SKIN IS WHEN
YOUR REAL BEAUTY
SHINES THROUGH.'

THE IMPORTANCE OF A BRA THAT FITS PROPERLY

We've dressed hundreds of women between us, and of all of them, only one woman was wearing the right-sized bra. We gave her a trophy — well, we like to recognise when you get it right! But if so many are getting it wrong, how do we fix the problem?

The first thing to do is to find a good professional bra fitter, which can be easier said than done. A key to how serious your retailer is about bra fitting is the range of sizes that they stock. A good specialist supplier will start with back size 28 and go up to 48. This avoids the potential pitfall of being sold a size that isn't correct, just because it's in stock.

Some fitters use a tape, some don't: don't be put off by either approach, the proof is how well the bra fits.

WHAT IS THE ESSENCE OF A WELL-FITTING BRA?

There are three ways to ensure a well-fitting bra and they must be put in place in the right order. The first thing to get right is the *back size*. The back strap of your bra should sit neat, low and straight across the back. If it bows upwards, it is too big.

Most women wear their bras at least two inches too big on the back. Often, a smaller back fit can feel odd at first, but bear with us; it's just because you're not used to wearing the proper fit.

Once the back is in place, you can begin to choose the *cup size*. If you've gone down one back size, you'll need to go up at least one cup size from the one you normally wear. You will know it's right when the centrepiece of the bra sits flush to the skin in between your boobs and the cups envelop your boobs neatly without them spilling over the top. Finally, but importantly, adjust the shoulder straps to bring the *bust line* to that hallowed spot half-way between the shoulder and the elbow.

Here, our bra expert **CLODAGH WEBER** from specialist lingerie store, Bramora, gives you the benefit of her expertise on all things bra-related . . .

As over ninety per cent of women in Ireland are wearing the incorrect bra size, it is so important to be properly fitted by professionals. It is also important to have this done regularly — twice a year is about right. A lot of ladies guess their own size rather than going to be fitted and this is where a lot of the problems lie. Fitting is something that should only take a few minutes and will make you feel and look so much better when you are finished! Most importantly, your clothes will look so much better on you too!

I myself have had bad experiences in the past, which is why Bramora was born. I would go from one place to another and be told I was a different size in different shops. Having now been in business for nearly seven years, we still see the same problems coming through the door every day. We always endeavour to sort each and every lady out and it has been our aim to make women look and feel better about themselves. A correctly fitting bra can make all the difference to your shape, making you look slimmer and your breasts smaller, or bigger, whatever the case may be!

There are many questions we get asked by customers, but here are some of the most common:

1. What is the 'band' and what is the 'cup'?

2. Why are my breasts spilling out of the cup?

3. How do I get rid of this back fat?

4. Why is the bra riding up my back?

5. Why are my shoulders so sore from ridges?

6. Why are my breasts sitting so low?

7. How will I know if it is fitting me right?

8. I don't like to wear a wired bra as it hurts. Why?

ANSWERS:

1. The 'band' of a bra is the 30, 32, 34, 36 measurement, i.e., your back size, and the 'cup' is the breast size, A, B, C, D, DD and so on.

2. If your breasts are spilling out over the top of your bra, this means that the cup size is far too small. You need to go bigger on the cup size by one or two sizes. If the back feels firm enough, leave it alone. (Most ladies have one breast bigger than the other, so always make sure that the bigger breast is totally encased in the cup — the other side may be a little puckered, but this will fill out once worn for a while.)

3. Back fat is something that most, if not all, ladies have to deal with, and the reason why so many are wearing incorrectly fitting bras is because they think going up a band size is the answer when, in fact, it's the opposite. The band of the bra needs to be firm (but not too tight) as this is where all the support in the bra is! So, ladies, if you are very conscious of back fat, maybe try a wider band rather than a bigger one!

4. When a bra is riding up the back, this is simply because the band going around your back is far too big. If your cup size fits OK, just come down in the band size but make sure to go up a cup size — for example, if you are finding that a 36E is fitting OK on the cup but is riding

LINDA WALSH, CORK

LINDA LYONS,
GALWAY

'BEAUTY IS A HAPPY, CONFIDENT PERSON WHO IS COMFORTABLE IN THEMSELVES AND WITH THEIR APPEARANCE. I RECENTLY LOST 13 STONE. I AM A HAPPY MOTHER OF TWO BOYS AND HAVE A WONDERFUL HUSBAND.'

up on the back, change to a 34F — this should make all the difference.

5. Ridges are caused from the bra being too big in the band and therefore all the support is being taken in the shoulders. Try going down a few back sizes and up in the cup sizes.

6. If your breasts are sitting quite low and they feel like they need a lift sometimes it is as easy as adjusting the straps. Your breasts should be sitting half-way between your shoulder and your elbow: NO LOWER!! When the breasts are nice and pert, they make you look slimmer and show off your figure so much better. Sometimes, however, it can be that again the band of the bra you are wearing is too loose, so just go smaller on the back and bigger in the cup. This should sort it out.

7. If a bra is fitting correctly, the band will fit firmly around the back, but not too tight, and the cup of the bra will totally cover the full breast so that nothing is spilling out (if too small) or digging in (if too big). And the breasts should be sitting nicely between the shoulder and the elbow.

8. If you are turned off by wires in a bra, this is usually because the bra simply does not fit. The wires are digging in as the cup is too small and this turns people off as it is hurting. All you need to change is the cup size — if the band feels OK then stick with it, but just adjust the cup size upwards by a few sizes and this will work for you.

Finally, it's ideal to have a good every-day bra in your lingerie drawer, a good multiway or strapless bra and, if necessary, a good sports bra. Sports bras are so important to have, even if your daily exercise is just walking.

All these are just guidelines. Getting professionally fitted is the most important thing, for every lady.

YOUR UNDERWEAR CAPSULE WARDROBE

Your drawer of smalls should be organised to offer all the solutions you need for your lifestyle. So, what are the essential elements for this collection? Consider the pieces as allies, with different roles to play, even different personalities . . .

WHAT	WHO	WHEN
Nude moulded t-shirt bra	The reliable geek	Any old day
Black moulded t-shirt bra	The reliable geek with notions	Any old day plus
The stretch lace bra	The femme fatale	The low-level special occasion
The multi-way	The whizz kid	When confronted by a challenging dress

And, while it might sound a little old fashioned, there's something lovely about wearing matching underwear: it makes you feel in control, and it's easier to achieve than you might think. When compiling your underwear capsule collection, buy three pairs of matching knickers for each bra and you should be guaranteed that feel-good factor daily.

A before and after shot of our lovely model. Notice the difference? She's peachy with the proper fit.

YOUR CAPSULE WARD-ROBE:

WORKHORSES TO SHOW PONIES

WE ONCE DID AN INTERESTING IF SLIGHTLY SCARY EXERCISE WITH ONE OF OUR GORGEOUS CANDIDATES, THE WONDERFUL MAG O'LEARY DOYLE. MAG WON'T MIND ME SAYING THAT HER PURCHASING HABITS WERE BORDERING ON OBSESSIVE (SHE ADMITTED IT HERSELF IN FRONT OF THE NATION). WHAT MAG HAD FALLEN INTO WAS A HABIT OF REPETITIVE PURCHASING: TWENTY PAIRS OF TRACKSUIT BOTTOMS, FIFTEEN PAIRS OF METALLIC HIGH HEELS, MANY UNWORN. AND IT WENT ON.

WHEN WE ASKED Mag to tot up how much she'd spent on all the items she'd purchased, it was a rude awakening. And yet, Mag is not alone: so many women buy variations on a theme of continuous monotony without relating the purchase to how it fits into the wardrobe you already have and what's in it.

Imagine you were sick of cooking the same meals over and over again. You want to try something new but you keep buying the same ingredients. So you keep making the same food. This is a lot like what happens in our wardrobes until we get to the point where we have loads of clothes and nothing to wear.

So, it's time for the plan. For us and the women we serve, it's all about creating solutions. Easy options that make you feel like you look good doing the school run. These solutions are basically the elements of the Fully Functioning Wardrobe, more commonly known as the Capsule Wardrobe. The Capsule Wardrobe expresses a perfect balance between what we call Workhorses and Show Ponies. If that sounds like a stretched analogy, stay with us, it makes perfect sense.

WORKHORSES

These little darlings are the hard grafters. They are what you reach for when you don't have enough time to check whether yesterday's knickers are still in your jeans! It has happened. . .

The nature of workhorses is that they are subtle solutions for everyday life. For that reason, choose pieces in dark and light neutral colours. We urge you to think outside of the black trap and build your wardrobe around your choice of brown, grey or navy for dark colours and subtle ivory, cream, stone and dove grey for contrast. The more subtle the colours, the more wear you will get out of your new wardrobe.

Workhorses include the following:

A MULTIFUNCTIONAL 'SLEEPER' DRESS

This is a dress that you can wear again and again and no-one will even notice. It has chameleon qualities, allowing it to move from boardwalk to boardroom with the addition of some choice accessories.

The sleeper dress should always be in a dark neutral colour, in a fabric that doesn't respond badly to drool or toothpaste. It should be chosen for how flattering it is to your body shape. This is a dress that will subtly show off what you've got and conceal any gripes or issues. Because of its innate simplicity, it can sustain the addition of any combination of the following:

SHIRT   CARDIGAN
T-SHIRT   STRUCTURED JACKET
BLOUSE   STATEMENT JEWELLERY
BELT

A SKIRT

Much like the dress and indeed all items within the capsule wardrobe, the shape must be specifically chosen to flatter your form. Dark neutral is the preference in colour. If your hip and thigh area is the problem, skirts can be the solution. Move away from jeans and trousers and find comfort in a high-waisted full skirt. All you curvy hourglasses need to own a pencil skirt; rulers and apples, play with tulip shapes to rebalance the silhouette.

TROUSERS

The best trousers for you are hard won, and should offer you a flattering shape, durability and a range of ways to wear them. If you are long waisted, you're going to need a higher 'rise' (the distance from the crotch to the natural waist). If you are short in the rise, hipster styles can suit as they graze the natural waist. If your legs are short, whether in proportion or not, go for the longest leg length that you can comfortably handle. The baggy ³/₄ length trousers, so favoured in Ireland as a casual staple, do little for even the slimmest frame.

Oh, you are all very vocal on the issue of jeans. Well, we've done a lot of research in the area and know how to choose the right pair for your shape: stay with us through the photo-shoot and shopping directory. Avoid the temptation to go oversized. Try and stay as neat to your form as you find comfortable. Our advice: don't even think about buying jeans without a stretch composition. Muffin top can easily be avoided by lengthening the rise, and favouring high-waisted styles. It takes a little getting used to, but gives a much more streamlined look.

A SHORT, STRUCTURED JACKET

Tailoring has the magic power to create wonderful structure in the silhouette. The mind-shift comes when you realise that a jacket isn't valuable simply for practical purposes, but for its use as a silhouette-balancer. No matter that it won't keep you warm, or even that it closes, in fact, an open jacket can create a wonderfully slimming line.

AN OUTER JACKET

An outer jacket is the practical cousin of the structured jacket. It should create great structure in the silhouette but has the added duty of providing warmth. Your outer jacket should be a garment of some distinction.

TRENCH

Your choice of trench, as ever, comes down to your body shape, and unlike the short jacket, serves a practical purpose, depending on your lifestyle requirements. If your main forays into public involve trips to the opera, red-carpet events and openings, something dramatic and luxurious will be required. If, on the other hand, like the rest of us, there are kids or dogs to be walked, driven to park or school and groceries to be bought, a coat is required that has warmth and practicality. For many of us, that means resorting to the ubiquitous down-filled jacket or puffa. Please, know that there is another way!

EMMA DEVINE, MULLINGAR

'BEAUTY IS HAVING A PERSONALITY AND THE ABILITY TO HOLD YOUR OWN IN THE COMPANY OF OTHERS. I AM BEAUTIFUL BECAUSE I AM NICE TO PEOPLE AND VERY OUTGOING. I AM GOOD COMPANY TO BE IN AND I TRY TO MAKE THE MOST OF WHAT I HAVE BEEN GIVEN!'

TOPS

Be aware that practicality doesn't have to devour style, and often layering is a more effective way to address the issue of keeping warm in this country. P.S. It doesn't *have* to be black.

Looking around, you may be led to believe that fleeces are standard issue in Ireland. If you want to mask any sense of self behind a rectangular wall of brightly coloured recycled polymers, go ahead. Just don't tell us that it makes you feel good about yourself, because we don't believe you. Far better, we believe, to push yourself into making an effort, and grow a sense of respect and enjoyment for you and your clothes. 'Tops' is a broad category, including the following:

T-SHIRTS   TUNICS

SHIRTS   SHELLS

BLOUSES   VESTS

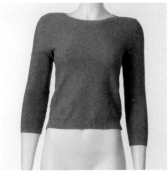

Beautiful tactile knitwear can be a great ally in our unfriendly climate. Layering is the key to warmth and comfort and the ever-changing moods of the Irish weather.

In years gone by, it would have sounded extraordinarily extravagant to prescribe cashmere as a wardrobe staple. However, it is now mass produced and widely available, most notably through such high-street stalwarts as Marks & Spencer. Not only does it offer great warmth without bulk, it also feels *so* wonderful against the skin that once smitten, many find themselves unable to return to lesser yarns.

Cashmere thickness is counted in 'ply' and can come in anything from an ultra-lightweight T-shirt to a heavy outer knit, but be warned: the heavier the ply, the heftier the price tag.

So that's the beginning of you being able to take control of your wardrobe. With all these well-chosen elements in place, you have the building blocks of a fully functioning wardrobe. What you need now is the glue to put them together.

SHOW PONIES

Of course the basics are important, and we can't begin this process without them. But what really gets us all excited is the gilding. The clever style queen uses this to elevate a look, to create a personal signature and maximise the potential of those workhorses. So many women have spoken to us about their inability to accessorise. You only have to look at the very in-vogue Wallis Simpson to see the practice elevated to an art form. Although, a personal collection of Cartier fine jewellery would put a smile on most women's faces!

If the workhorse's job is to fade into the background, then the show pony's job is to create a splash. Don't shy away from colour, pattern and texture. For the braver among us, push yourself to sparkles, sequins and spangles (whatever they are!); after all, this is the fun bit. Colour and pattern can be scary for the uninitiated and the cautious: bringing these elements into your new wardrobe with accessories is a gentle solution and a lesser investment.

On the facing page is a little smorgasbord of the gilding available to us. One thing that we have learned is that you can have the most divine accessories in the world, but if you can't see them, you won't wear them. Storage of your accessories is paramount, preferably in clear boxes or pouches. There are lots of storage solutions out there, from Penneys to home-storage specialists Howards Storage World and Muji. Just identify what's right for you and your budget.

EARRINGS

Of course there are workhorse earrings, delicate darlings that stay with us every day. For gilding, we're more interested in a statement. Don't forget that every shape we choose affects the overall silhouette we create. If your face is round, keep the earring shape long and lean. If your face is long you can afford to go short and wide with the earrings.

NECKLACES

The emphasis is again on shape. A long necklace will draw the eye down, but don't be tempted to go lower than the bust line if you're curvy, as the necklace will hang off the widest point of the bust. Rulers and Pears: statement necklaces worn high on the collarbone are a great rebalancing aid.

BROOCHES AND PINS

These can be a great way to individualise your style and work well with vintage-inspired looks.

RINGS

Of course if you have elegant piano-playing fingers, you can choose to wear delicate or oversized finger adornments. If, however, your fingers are big, choose bigger rings to keep the balance right. A delicate ring will make your fingers seem bigger.

SHOES

So often the holy grail of accessories for the style hungry, shoes are fun to buy and a great way to update your wardrobe. Balance (in more ways then one) is everything. Too high now looks a little wrong, and while a subtle platform is a great way to lengthen the leg without pain, too deep and you risk looking like a drag act. If your legs are in any way big, go for a block heel to keep the proportions balanced.

Coloured footwear is great for updating your looks and is a good start to free you from the black trap.

BOOTS

You can choose your boots to be practical or not. Every wardrobe should have a good flat and heeled pair to choose from. Don't automatically go for black — grey, navy and brown make for rich and useful companions. Beware the 'boot gap'

when wearing skirts; a boot top disappearing under the hem of a skirt is a great look.

HANDBAGS

Oversized or micro bag, or anything in between: the choice is yours. If you're petite, try to avoid a bag so big that it looks like your living quarters. A good day bag should be comfortable and not too heavy. Tan, navy, brown and stone are good colour choices.

GLOVES

For occasion wear, leather gloves can really add a touch of old-school glamour to your look. Time was when a woman would not be seen leaving the house without this finishing touch.

SCARVES

Scarves are perhaps the most daunting but most useful accessories in our arsenal. Trust us, they're not just for keeping your neck warm. Neckerchief to oversized wrap, practice makes perfect for the uninitiated. The masters, Hermès, have some wonderful tips for tying scarves online.

STOLES

Stoles are considered the more lavish cousin to the scarf. Feathery, furry, cashmere or sequinned they are the ultimate gilding for occasion wear.

BELTS

In Lennon-Courtney Towers, we can't overstate the defining powers of the belt. So many women are scared to trust in those powers but trust us. Try belting cardigans and jackets, dresses and coats, we promise you, you won't be disappointed. Let belts be your foray into colour. And don't go too wide unless the 80s are calling you.

AVRIL KEYS, BELFAST

'I THINK I AM BEAUTIFUL BECAUSE I DON'T WEAR TOO MUCH MAKE-UP, I KEEP IT NATURAL. I'M A MUM BUT STILL HAVE MY OWN IDENTITY. I DON'T TAKE FASHION/ BEAUTY SERIOUSLY. I'VE LEARNED TO BECOME CONFIDENT IN MY OWN SKIN AND BE HAPPY WITH WHAT I HAVE NOW. AFTER SPENDING MY 20S AND EARLY 30S OVERLY CRITICAL OF MYSELF, I WISH I HAD THE CONFIDENCE I HAVE NOW WHEN I WAS 20!'

HATS

Hats come in so many incarnations that there is categorically one for everyone. If you're petite, it figures that a wide brim is going to create a mushroom effect, so proceed with caution. Fascinators are now facing a ban at certain events – we think it's time to let them go, particularly when the wonderful world of hats is there to explore.

TIGHTS

One of the least expensive investments in your wardrobe can represent the most fun in terms of self expression. Colour and pattern can be a great way to personalise your look. Co-ordinating coloured tights and matching shoes is the ultimate way to lengthen the leg.

COLOUR CHALLENGE

Gorgeous Shannon came to us as a self-confessed black-trap victim. Of course, we had to rise to the challenge. With Shannon's striking colouring and features, this canary yellow jacket was a bold move but one that was greeted by hoots of approval from all in attendance, not least by Shannon herself. Another happy customer.

CHAPTER 5

YOUR BEST YOU

SO HERE WE ARE, HOMEWORK DONE, IT'S TIME TO SEE HOW OUR ADVICE WORKS IN REAL LIFE. OUR FOUR GORGEOUS LADIES GET FIVE KEY LOOKS, BASED ON THEIR SHAPES AND LIFESTYLES. HOURGLASS, PEAR, RULER, APPLE, THERE'S A LOOK FOR EVERY ASPECT OF THEIR BUSY LIVES: DOWN TIME, DAY TIME, WORK TIME, PARTY TIME AND SHOW TIME. IT'S ALL THERE FOR YOU TO ENJOY. WE HOPE THEY'LL INSPIRE YOU.

HOURGLASS ⊠

- To show you how work wear can have a real feel-good factor, we've thrown the cat amongst the pigeons and gone for red for Wendy's professional look. Because we've gone for separates instead of a dress, Wendy has more possibilities with these pieces. She can split them to create different looks for different pieces of the lifestyle pie chart: top with jeans for Day Time, skirt with sheer blouse for Party Time.

- When proportions are good, as with all hourglasses, dressing has to be a 'camouflage-free zone'. If you hide that waist, you conceal (one of) your best assets. Plus, billowing tops will hang down from the widest point of the bust, making the gorgeous hourglass seem much bigger than she is.

- The high-necked top is balanced by the short sleeve, giving the perfect combination of conceal and reveal. The delicate gathering in the shoulder accentuates the waist, as does the belt. The stark red is softened with tan accessories.

- The pencil skirt was created to show off Wendy's hourglass curves, and hits that perfect point just below the knee.

- The tan courts are perfect leg-lengtheners, a wardrobe classic and also act as true footwear workhorses.

DOWN TIME

- Down Time can present big problems for curvy girls. Often, when the structure of tailoring is taken away, so too is definition of the silhouette. In this look, we've softened everything but retained the waist with this belted top.

- Stripes can be scary but once you retain the waistline, there's no cause for alarm.

- We've replaced Wendy's trusty jeans with cropped carrot-leg trousers in a soft tan colour. These are a true wardrobe workhorse for our hourglass sirens: you only have to think Marilyn Monroe to get the tried-and-tested style.

- Ballet pumps offer a feminine option in a flat shoe and it turns out that a little well-placed bling can be quite the mood-enhancer.

- For a look to cover anything from the school run to lunch with the girls, Wendy is sporting clothes that are the perfect marriage of comfort, style and figure flattery. Building on soft neutrals, we maximise the opportunity to create looks that whisper rather than shout. Accent comes in the form of the print of the blouse and the tan belt.

- The long-line cardigan and blouse are saved from falling into the camouflage trap with our trusty belt.

- Of course, given the volume on the top, we have to create balance with these cropped skinny jeans.

- We know this look would work with the ballet flats, but we couldn't resist the classic court to lift this look (literally) to another level.

PARTY TIME

- For Party Time, we've pushed Wendy into the limelight with this great sculpted dress. Not everyone can wear this colour, but it's worth finding out how far you can push yourself, and in what direction, with colour: a bold or unexpected colour pop can really have a wow factor.

- In terms of definition, this dress is doing all the right things, out at the shoulders, in at the waist, out at the hips. The comfort of the pleating detail on the skirt could work well for a pear shape, too, but in a darker colour.

- We've teamed the dress with leggings to give a more relaxed feel to the look.

- Ankle boots are a great way to give a contemporary slant to your look and are a true footwear workhorse.

- All hourglass babes out there, we urge you to use those curves! This dress is by Vivienne Westwood and gives some old-school glamour to Wendy's fabulous figure.

- Pattern and print create accent in our wardrobe but can create their own problems. Oversized prints must be woven into a sculpted form or you risk the 'tent' effect.

- The classic court is a low-key way to complete the look; nothing more is needed.

HOURGLASS DOS AND DON'TS

- **DO** be proud of your perfectly womanly 'figure of 8'
- **DO** define your waist at every opportunity
- **DO** high-waisted skirts and trousers, they will give you the tummy support you crave
- **DO** allow yourself to feel sexy

- **DON'T** do too many layers, they'll swamp those gorgeous curves
- **DON'T** do A-line, instead go for bell-shape skirts and remember, the pencil skirt was made for you.
- **DON'T** do high-neck anything, particularly if you have big boobs

PEAR

- With our gorgeous pears, the mission is to rebalance the hip-to-shoulder ratio, making the shoulders appear bigger. Always keep darker colours to the lower half with brightness or lightness up top.

- These soft carrot-leg trousers are set to become Louise's best friend. The volume on the hips and thigh creates gentle camouflage and the tapering leg creates balance.

- The eye is drawn up by the stone and yellow top which would be a hard-working asset to any wardrobe.

- Finally, the shoulders are balanced with a classic blazer, neatly cropped with a flattering bracelet sleeve.

- The multi-tasking ankle boot, this time in stone, gives the look a contemporary edge.

DOWN TIME

- This tobacco jacket provides a great bit of structure for Down Time, the belted detail drawing the eye in to the waist.

- The victim of gross over-exposure, we still love a Breton top (just not when everyone's wearing them).

- Jeans are the staple of the Down Time uniform, but often for our gorgeous pears, they're close to impossible to get right. Anything low rise will accentuate the hips, which is not what we want. So, if you're not going low — go high! Follow your waist up to its narrowest point, showing off its narrowness, because Pear lovelies have great waists. This has the added effect of getting rid of the 'muffin top'. You'll be surprised how proud you can be of your bootylicious rear when the jeans are right.

- Tommy Hilfiger 'Paris' jeans have never failed to impress our Perfect Pears.

WORK TIME

- Suiting doesn't have to mean a jacket: what's important is that we create structure. It also doesn't have to be dark and boring. This two-piece almost does the job of a dress, but the good news is you can buy the top and bottom in different sizes. All you Pears know that your bottom half is a minimum of one size bigger than your top half, so this makes for a simple solution to the problem.

- The gentle puff shoulder on the blouse gives us our slight over-extension, and the waistcoat defines the waist beautifully.

- 'Tulip' shaped skirts are often seen as dangerous territory for reluctant Pears but actually, they're the ideal shape for our curvy-hipped friends: the key is in the fact that the skirt narrows at the knee.

- Nude courts are no longer a secret, but they remain the best way to lengthen the leg.

- If there's one era dedicated to our Pear gals, it's the 1950s. No drama about the top half fitting and the bottom half not — you can delight in your narrow upper half with abandon. With that in mind, the bright royal blue looks great with Louise's fair complexion.

- If you're looking for a jacket to put over this creation, remember to stay neat to the waist with either a crop or peplum shape.

- We've gone cutesy with a flat pump, but equally, an elegant court would look killer.

- It's not all about retro styling: some clever colour-blocking can accent and conceal admirably, if chosen correctly. Remember, bright or light colours on top, deeper colours down low.

- All the key detail on this great dress is happening above the waist. The asymmetric batwing sleeve and sneaky reveal of Louise's lean arm (a common pear asset) mean that the eye is drawn unwaveringly up.

PEAR DOS AND DON'TS

- **DO** skim your hips when it comes to trousers and skirts

- **DO** use darker tones to distract from the bits you don't like

- **DO** use detail and brighter tones to highlight what you do like

- **DO** remember its all about balance with you

- **DON'T** over-emphasise your waist, it will make your hips look bigger

- **DON'T** be afraid to try a pencil skirt; if it's cut well, it can work

- **DON'T** wear shapeless baggy clothes, you will look bigger

- **DON'T** be ruled by what your mother told you, try on everything

APPLE

- A trench coat is a great weapon in the battle to look stylish off duty. It's a cover-all and a classic wardrobe workhorse.

- We've utilised a cowl neckline on Mary, in an accent graphic print.

- Skinny jeans! Mary's new best friend. In a dark dye they can look really smart and ever so flattering on our gorgeous Apple's lean legs.

- These pumps have a little block heel, so comfort and additional height are on offer.

DAY TIME

- Luscious Apples, you now know who you are. Our main aim is to cleverly conceal that torso and tummy, while releasing the glory of your limbs.

- We've given Mary a starter palette of blues and navies. Importantly, the top is bright blue and the cardigan is navy, creating a very slimming effect. The draped cowl on the top draws the eye down to the waist, made narrower by the darker cardigan. Even the self belt on the top is an important detail, further defining the waist. The volume in the cardigan is balanced with the narrow sleeve.

- Mary is showing off those pins in navy capri pants. Again, it's all about balance. The key is to go high-waisted to minimise lumps and bumps.

- We know we could have gone with flats, but hey! It's Mary's moment.

WORK TIME

- A well-tailored shirt dress is the perfect boardroom staple: smart, sassy and above all, easy to wear.

- It provides maximum punch for the workplace, but will keep Mary feeling confident and stylish.

- A tonal tight adds personality.

- Draping and cut help define Mary's waist, while colour keeps the look fresh and fun.

- Above the knee means party time and also shows off Mary's stunning pins.

- Coloured tights add interest while maintaining elegance.

- For party time, it's heels all the way. No excuses!

- The positive effect of draping and print is used to its best advantage in this dress. Everything brings the eye into the centre point of Mary's waist. While the print is bold, the colours are muted, but bold and bright is one to watch, as it is possible to have too much of a good thing.

- This dress would take a jacket very well, just be careful to go for deep reveres and a narrow point of connection, echoing the magic that the dress is working.

APPLE DOS AND DON'TS

- **DO** find your waist. Your narrowest point is normally at the top of your rib cage

- **DO** showcase your lovely long limbs

- **DO** colour blocking and cleverly cut clothing to build a shape you love

- **DO** use jackets and coats as accessories to redefine your silhouette

- **DON'T** do double-breasted ANYTHING, it will just add bulk

- **DON'T** do oversized or slouchy clothes, they will add inches

- **DON'T** ever not wear the right size bra: your shape gets the most benefit from wearing the correct sized bra

RULER

- Look at this gorgeous creature! It's hard to feel any sympathy for Aoife's svelte figure; however, most rulers feel boyish and unfeminine, so our job is to inject some curves into that gorgeousness.

- This little sculpted jacket is a real multi-tasker and looks as good with jeans as it would in the workplace. Under it is a clever little peplum asymmetric top, creating curve at the hip.

- These skinny jeans are showing off the gentle curve of Aoife's own figure and could easily be replaced by carrot-leg trousers.

- We're building a really nice palette of soft neutrals with this look, in colours that Aoife had never considered before.

- Aoife's waist- and bust-line have been exaggerated by using this gathered and draped cardigan.

- Pale denim can be hard to work as you really have nowhere to hide, however a Ruler's legs are not for hiding.

- The tone is continued using these stone ankle boots, which also lengthens the leg (as if it needed lengthening!)

WORK TIME

- The volume in this clever dress is doing all the right things. The full skirt introduces hips and the gathering on the top accentuates Aoife's bust.

- We've added a crisp white shirt for that no-nonsense professional look, but this dress could do many different jobs in a clever girl's wardrobe.

- We've chosen navy courts, but boots would work equally well. Just make sure they are tall enough to disappear under the hemline.

- We love our pale complexions and see no reason to shy away from challenging colours. This peach pelmet dress is creating definition at the waist and curve at the hip.

- The flirtiness is offset by the tuxedo jacket, belted to maximise that waist.

- Volume, unsurprisingly, can create more volume and needs to be approached with caution. The key is in the art of conceal and reveal. This accordion pleated dress could, of course, be belted (great for pear and hourglass), but Aoife's svelte figure can sustain the beautiful flow of it loose.

- Again, we've chosen navy over black as colour for this key piece, because it's much kinder on pale skin tones.

- And for accent, a pop of colour in the shoes and a statement necklace.

RULER DOS AND DON'TS

- **DO** look for clothes that build curves and create interest, everything from tailoring to draping
- **DO** pay particular attention to building detail on the hips and shoulders
- **DO** use lots of layering
- **DO** remember you are the envy of all your friends

- **DON'T** be afraid of bold prints, you can totally rock them
- **DON'T** do dropped waists, they will ruin your proportion
- **DON'T** forget, there is actually not a lot you can't wear

CHAPTER 6

THE ART OF SHOPPING

HOW DO YOU FEEL ABOUT CLOTHES SHOPPING?

NIAMH DEMPSEY, *OFF THE RAILS*, SEASON 8:

'I HATED IT, I AVOIDED SHOPPING AS MUCH AS POSSIBLE. WHENEVER I REALLY NEEDED SOMETHING, IT WAS A SNATCH-AND-GRAB JOB. I NEVER LOOKED AT THE SIZE OR THE STYLE, ONCE IT WAS BIG AND USUALLY A DARK COLOUR, I GENERALLY GRABBED IT.'

NOW, THAT DOESN'T sound like fun. Makeover candidates have gone so far as to say they've experienced drying in the mouth and feelings of deep anxiety when approaching a shop. The negative associations run very deep, and they have a lot to do with body image and confidence; however, there's more to it than that. The reason that this book will be so valuable to you in taking control of your image is that it will arm you with the appropriate knowledge to understand how to shop successfully.

THE SHOPPING MYTH

There are certainly a few among us who love shopping . . . and then there are the rest of us, to whom we like to fondly refer as 'delusional' shoppers.

A delusional shopper is a shopper who thinks they like shopping when actually they only like shopping for stuff that they find non-threatening . . . When we look at them more closely, we can actually gently categorise them. We have the . . .

SHOES AND BAG SHOPPERS

Now, you're sitting up! So many women love to shop, but only for shoes and handbags, because buying them doesn't make you feel fat or question your appearance — it just feels good. There are many of you out there who have become so addicted to shoes and bags, we've had to wean you off this accessory addiction, like going cold turkey. You know who you are! Less dramatically, there are the women who 'just love shoes and bags', women who, while not quite *addicted* still experience an enormous opportunity cost to the rest of their wardrobe, because they are spending all their money on just two items: shoes and bags. And the more you spend on shoes and bags, the less you have for REAL clothes!! Don't get us wrong, we get your adoration for these little (or in the case of bags and, depending on trend, massively oversized) gems. But everything in moderation to get ultimate maximisation for your money and your wardrobe.

CHRISTINA CASSIDY, GALWAY

'BEAUTY IS CONFIDENCE AND FEELING COMFORTABLE IN YOUR OWN SKIN. I AM BEAUTIFUL BECAUSE I'VE EARNED EVERY YEAR OF MY WRINKLES AND AGEING AND HAVE LEARNED TO LIVE WITH AND APPRECIATE THEM!'

FOOD SHOPPERS

Again, you know who you are. You love to spend hundreds of euro on fancy food. After all, cooking is such a wonderful pastime, apart from its practical value. But there are women who over spend on food in order to avoid spending on themselves. And, of course, there are the obvious health pitfalls that go along with all that food.

PEOPLE WHO SHOP FOR OTHER PEOPLE

Every family has one. The perfect gift buyer, the person who has Christmas sorted by July. They are thoughtful and spend way too much on gifts. All this is good and they mean well, but often they are neglecting themselves or using spending on others as a way to avoid shopping for themselves. If you recognise yourself here, you'll know it's not good. It's just masking your own frustration with your wardrobe. Start spending on yourself.

Whether you see yourself in one of the categories above, the reality is, few of us actually love shopping *for ourselves*. Many of you feel so badly about your bodies that even going into a shop, let alone trying something on, can fill you with absolute dread and even panic in some cases. What a shame. And when you consider how hard you all work, you deserve to feel good about spending your hard-earned cash on yourselves.

But before we even get onto the subject of shopping, why not start with being nice to yourselves? Mothers tend to be the most selfless of creatures (just as nature intended) but there comes a point where if you are not happy, your children will not be happy. We really believe this. You must show your children how to be kind to themselves and that starts with them observing *you* being kind to yourself. So, before you even set foot in a shop, remember: BE NICE TO YOURSELF.

LET'S BEGIN BY SEEING IF SHOPPING IS WORKING FOR YOU

How do we turn around our challenges and insecurities and take control of our shopping habits? Like everything in life, knowledge has a huge role to play in how we approach the subject, and guess what happens when you have the knowledge? Your confidence grows in parallel. Let's look at the questions you need to consider about your shopping trip before you set out.

ARE YOU WINDOW-SHOPPING?

This is a valid pursuit. After all, how can you know what you want, if you don't do your research? If approached by a sales assistant, don't be afraid to let them know that you won't be spending today: it's your right to look. Consider it a reconnaissance mission; soak up the colours, trend stories and displays. We all have a budget range, but don't be afraid to window shop beyond that. If you can't aspire to it, you can't be inspired by it.

ARE YOU ON A MISSION?

Here, you feel there is a gap in your wardrobe, there's a particular item that you need, either for a special occasion or to make something else work. This can be the most difficult shopping task, because the more specific your requirement, the more difficult it can be to crack the mission. Unless you do your research . . . luckily, the internet is now a great way to see what's available, even if you still want the full retail experience. If you're not internet savvy, and even if you are, the greatest potential allies in your search are the sales staff. If they don't know what stock they carry, then ask to speak to the manager. If the manager doesn't know, leave.

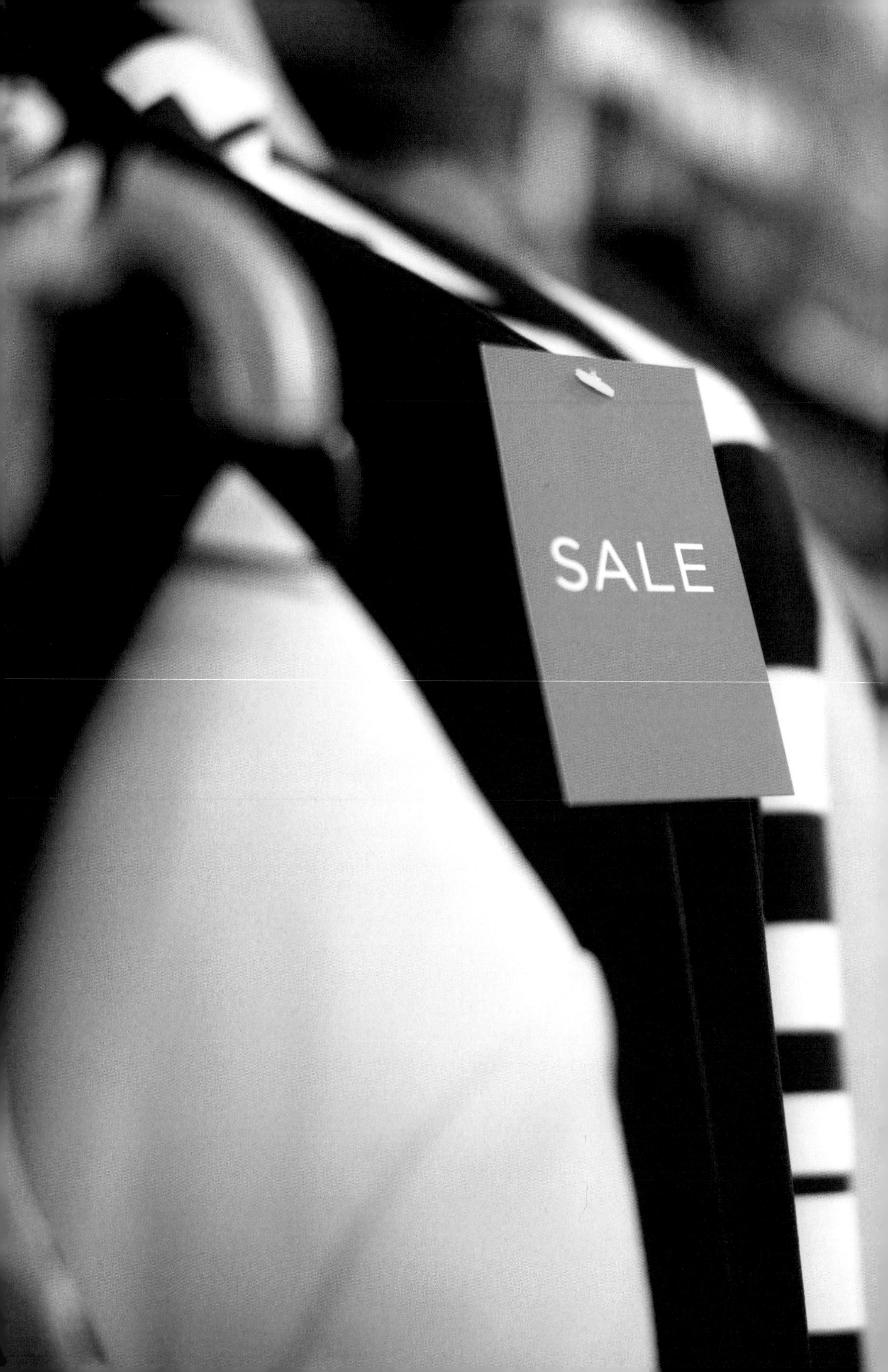
SALE

ARE YOU LOOKING FOR A RETAIL HIT?

For obvious reasons, this shopping pursuit is the most likely to lead to trouble. If you're ambling around, probably with a nominal amount of money to spend, it's very easy to do one of a few things:

> BUY SOMETHING THAT YOU ALREADY HAVE IN A SLIGHT VARIATION (BECAUSE YOU KNOW IT WORKS).
> GET SUCKED INTO THE LURE OF A BARGAIN. MORE ON THAT BELOW!
> FALL FOR THE WILDCARD AND BUY FOR THE LIFESTYLE YOU DON'T HAVE.
> FALL PREY TO BODY-IMAGE DELUSION AND BUY FOR THE BODY YOU DON'T HAVE. USING CLOTHES AS CARROTS FOR WEIGHT LOSS IS NEVER A GOOD IDEA.

ARE YOU LOOKING FOR A BARGAIN?

BARGAIN [bahr-guhn] Noun. *'An advantageous purchase, especially one acquired at less than the usual cost.'*

Oh, how we love a bargain. But so many 'bargains' turn out to be an unceremonious waste of money. We've discussed how those tagged-up garments in our wardrobes serve to remind us how little control we have over our human urges. Of all the questions to ask yourself before you buy, this is the most important, because our intellect is often clouded by the shiny lure of the bargain.

HAVE A GRAND PLAN OR 'THE SHOPPING MASTERPLAN'

Regardless of what type of shopping expedition you are planning, it's really important to have a plan. The plan is not about your bus route or how you're going to pay for the booty, it is about understanding the broad vision that you have for your fully functioning wardrobe and where your shopping choices fit into that.

The grand plan is developed by assessing our lifestyle needs, as per our lifestyle pie charts. Once we understand what we need in our wardrobes, we can then begin to think about what will make us look our best and therefore offer us the most value (regardless of price) in our collection. Ultimately, shopping should be fun, but it is easier to enjoy it when you know what you're doing.

SO HOW DO WE BEGIN TO TAKE CONTROL OF SHOPPING?

Like most things in life, preparation is everything. Before you dive aimlessly into a sea of fabric and unflattering lighting, remind yourself why you're in the shop in the first place. Earlier, we addressed the different types of shopping and suggested that you identify which type of adventure you're embarking on: window-shopping, mission shopping, random shopping or bargain shopping. Once you identify what you're trying to achieve, you can work out how to achieve it.

With your masterplan in place, see if you can answer the following messages:

CAN YOU READ THE STORE'S VISUAL MESSAGE?

For all but the very talented or very experienced, picking a personal 'edit', or selection, from thousands of items of stock is

SORCHA LOUGHREY, DUBLIN

'MY IDEA OF BEAUTY IS BEING COMFORTABLE IN ONE'S OWN SKIN. I'M FAR HAPPIER WITH MY SELF-IMAGE IN MY 30S THAN I EVER WAS BEFORE. I THINK THAT, AS MY SELF-CONFIDENCE HAS GROWN, I FEEL MORE BEAUTIFUL.'

a learned skill. The design of the retail space is a science based on constantly updated research. Retail designers encourage us through a pre-ordained pathway within the store: they decide which way we walk and what we are drawn to. They also endeavour to simplify the job by compartmentalising the stock into 'stories'. So, learning to read a store is a vital part of the shopping process.

To avoid that sense of feeling overwhelmed, break down the task into smaller parts. Rather than thinking of the store as a large cake, think of it as a box of chocolates. Each island or section will be themed, either work wear, party wear, or casual wear. Choose or reject each section individually based on what you're on the search for. By focusing on your mission you will be able to eliminate a large percentage of stock from the equation, making it so much easier to find what you're actually looking for.

HOW DO YOU PREPARE YOURSELF FOR THE TASK?

KAREN KEANE 'If I am going shopping I always wear a dress, tights and ballet flats. Easiest for pulling on and off, without being an ordeal.'

Karen, you're absolutely on the right track, preparation is everything. Pulling on and off skinny jeans, buckled shoes and re-layering can add to the pain of trying on, so simplify your outfit for 'quick-changeability'.

HOW DO YOU PICK WHAT TO TRY ON?

MAUREEN KEENAN: 'I hate that the rails are full of skinny-minnie clothes. There's very little choice for curvy women who love fashion. Black is not a colour!!! Grrrr, I could write an essay.'

HOW DO YOU MAKE THE MOST OF YOUR RELATIONSHIP WITH YOUR SALES ASSISTANT?

It might seem like an alien concept, but the sales assistant is there to help you make a purchase, that's part of his or her job description. It's time to get political. If you're not getting anywhere, go on a charm offensive, make human contact. Look around the store to find the friendliest face and engage. Tell your assistant of choice what you're looking for and if you feel you're drawing a blank, ask to speak to a manager. Ask the manager to suggest someone who can help or if she can help you herself. Even if the sales assistant doesn't have weekly targets, the manager certainly does, and your sale will help to reach them.

We need to grow our confidence in this arena and demand the service that we deserve.

Lots of you have told us that you are made to feel inferior and self-conscious by sales assistants in all manner of shopping environments. Quite often we project our own insecurities onto a situation. But much like the issue of sizing, there are huge inconsistencies in the approach of retail staff. Some are over eager, some are imperious. Ultimately, though, they are there to facilitate your shopping experience. So remember, you're in the driving seat, but your shopping experience very much depends on how well defined it is in your own head.

DO YOU TRY ON OR NOT?

EIMEAR DE SOUZA 'Not being allowed to take enough items into the changing room — I don't feel it reduces shoplifting (assuming that's what its purpose is). I need to take two sizes of everything in, due to variation between shops. Shops: I would buy more if I could try on more!'

For us, like Eimear, this is a serious issue. We'll warrant that all those tagged-up, unworn ghosts in your wardrobe are due to *not* trying things on. From this point on, that practice is not an option. When clothes shopping, you *must* try it on! We know it's painful, but if you want to spend your money efficiently and open the doors to your fully functioning wardrobe, three words apply: TRY IT ON. We can hear the sighs and groans as we speak. Don't worry, knowing how to approach this onerous task can ease the pain.

It's very easy, when you find that fabulous piece, to head straight to the fitting room with glee. Right there is where you stop and think! As we established, you're on a mission, of one sort or another. So, soldier, desist. Instead, grab a basket or even trolley if it's available (there's no shame: you're working towards your status as professional shopper!) and take the item you fancy, in the size you think you are, *and* the size up from that. Pull out as much as you like, you're the customer, remember that.

As Eimear says above, echoing the feelings of so many, the item-threshold for fitting rooms is an infuriating practice. However, from a stock-management point of view, it is unlikely to change.

The rule of thumb tends to be that the more you have to spend as a consumer, the more power you have to demand service. Unfortunate but true. (Things are changing though. The retailer wants and more than ever, *needs,* your money. So the power of the consumer is rising.) Now, you've already made friends with your sales assistant of choice, it's now time to enter into dialogue with the guardian of the fitting room. Look her straight in the eye and tell her that you are on a mission. You're not sure how their sizing works and so you've had to select two of everything. Ask her to hang onto the extra clothes while you take in the larger size in each garment and try it on. If it's too big, you can gloriously ask her would she mind passing in the smaller size (if you do it the other way round, it's not half as satisfying!).

HOW TO ENGAGE WITH YOUR RETAILER

REGISTER ONLINE WITH YOUR FAVOURITE STORE

Because retailers want your cash so badly, they are devising ingenious and valuable devices to entrap you in their worlds. Avoid the temptation to see this as a cynical exercise in greed, rather think of it as an opportunity for you to profit from their willingness to please you. Many sites, such as Topshop.com, offer an interactive voting system where online users can choose items of the week, and then go in-store to see the results. And online is not just about e-commerce: traditional retailers now see their websites as a valuable connection to their customers. It's also the ultimate communication tool, informing you of any value-added extras that your store may be offering, such as workshops, discounts and loyalty schemes. So don't be shy, sign up.

THE PERSONAL SHOPPER

Many stores have worked hard at installing personal shoppers and are providing a very good service. The value of a personal shopper cannot be underestimated. One of the pitfalls of shopping, which we've already discussed, is that we find ourselves in a loop of buying versions of the same thing. It's very hard to break that cycle without some form of external catalyst. That's how our makeover candidates can make the shift, by getting advice on thinking outside the box.

Unfortunately, we can't work with everyone in person, but personal shoppers can be a great alternative.

The basic premise requires that you enter into the process with an open mind. There's no point in making an appointment with a personal shopper if you're only going to consider what you would have bought anyway. Now, we know that this is a scary concept — it represents a loss of control, right? Wrong. The personal shopper isn't going to reach into your purse and divest you of your credit card; you're in the driving seat.

HOW TO SHOP ONLINE

Online shopping is increasingly becoming a reality of modern life: even the most technophobic among us have bought flights online. So, it's really a case of jump aboard or get left behind. But the one immutable truth of internet shopping is this:

IF IT LOOKS TOO GOOD TO BE TRUE, IT PROBABLY IS TOO GOOD TO BE TRUE.

The internet is awash with fakery and nowhere more does the term *caveat emptor* apply.

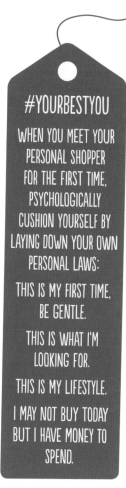

#YOURBESTYOU

WHEN YOU MEET YOUR PERSONAL SHOPPER FOR THE FIRST TIME, PSYCHOLOGICALLY CUSHION YOURSELF BY LAYING DOWN YOUR OWN PERSONAL LAWS:

THIS IS MY FIRST TIME, BE GENTLE.

THIS IS WHAT I'M LOOKING FOR.

THIS IS MY LIFESTYLE.

I MAY NOT BUY TODAY BUT I HAVE MONEY TO SPEND.

'BEAUTY IS WHAT
YOU MAKE OF
IT. I THINK I AM
BEAUTIFUL
BECAUSE I TRY TO
BE GOOD EVERY
DAY.'

HERE ARE A FEW TIPS ON HOW TO SHOP SAFELY ON THE INTERNET.

- *Only shop on reputable websites. So, the biggies that we've all heard of; going off-road is risky.*

- *Give the website a once-over, read the small print and then read the smaller print.*

- *Check that the site has a padlock at the bottom and starts with https, that means that it's secure and bona fide.*

- *Set up a PayPal account to ensure secure transactions, particularly with eBay, although it has broad applications.*

- *Never give your bank account details.*

- *Protect your credit card details with your provider's security service, Verified for Visa and Securecode for Mastercard.*

- *Never purchase on a public computer and if other people use the same terminal, be sure to log out when finished.*

- *Check the terms of your credit card provider. Some give additional services, such as purchase insurance for transactions over €100.*

So, armed with this information, it's time to go out there and get shopping! And to realise that as the consumer, you have the power. If you have money to spend, you cannot underestimate how important you are in the retail landscape. You only have to look at the valued-added offerings that retailers are concocting to make us part with our cash these days: in-store fashion shows and workshops, interactive websites, free personal shopping services and special discounts. If the staff on the ground can't follow through the message, take it higher. Remember, all these initiatives are to make you feel loved.

GILDING THE LILY:

CHAPTER 7

THE MAGIC OF HAIR AND MAKE-UP

'A WOMAN WHOSE SMILE IS OPEN AND WHOSE EXPRESSION IS GLAD HAS A KIND OF BEAUTY NO MATTER WHAT SHE WEARS.' ANNE ROIPHE

WE BELIEVE THAT beauty is in the eye of the beholder and that real beauty comes from within. But it's safe to say that the modern concept of 'beauty' is dictated to us: the idea that to be beautiful is to be young and skinny is pushed down our throats daily.

Well, we are very much at the forefront of a new and confident movement that celebrates age, curves and all ideas of beauty and for one reason only — reality. And that reality is that the vast majority of us aren't skinny models or celebrities. So, look around you and open your eyes and you will see real beauty everywhere.

That doesn't mean to say that we can't give nature a hand to enhance what we've got — with the right haircare and make-up. In this chapter, we look at just that — how to make the most of our natural assets, as part of *Your Best You*.

But before we do any of that, let's start with the canvas and give you some essential advice on looking after your skin.

Irish women tend to think about our national skin tone in negative terms: that it's pale or pasty. We disagree. Irish skin is wonderfully delicate in its natural form and should be thought of as an asset. Obviously, not all of us are pale faced, but whatever your skin type, the important thing is to protect what you've got. Our facial skin is our calling card to the world. A glowing complexion is shorthand for a healthy lifestyle and alert mind.

We believe that an investment in time and/or money in the preservation of our skin is very well spent. To that end, we both believe in regular facials and a regime of care and protection to help us keep what we've got in as good shape as possible. Of course, we'd rather you heard this from the experts than from us, mere recipients of their care and expertise. Over to you RACHEL WALSH of Sanctum Clinic! (www.sanctum.ie)

In Sanctum we work on the principle that creating and maintaining great skin requires an holistic approach — good topical products and treatments, combined with natural health strategies to reinforce the body and treat the underlying source of skin problems. You wouldn't build a house without foundations, so likewise, beautiful skin comes from good nutrition, to feed the skin from the inside out.

Here are my skincare secrets to help you realise beautiful skin at home.

DAILY SKIN COMMANDMENTS

› BEAUTIFUL SKIN REQUIRES A LITTLE DAILY LOVING CARE WITH PRODUCTS THAT ARE COMPATIBLE WITH YOUR SKIN TYPE. OUR SKIN IS A DYNAMIC ORGAN, CHANGING ACCORDING TO THE TIME OF YEAR AND THE CHALLENGES OF DAILY LIFE SO IT'S IMPORTANT TO LOOK AT WHAT YOUR SKIN NEEDS ON A DAILY BASIS — DON'T GET STUCK IN A RUT, USING THE SAME PRODUCTS MONTH ON MONTH, YEAR ON YEAR.

› MAKE AN APPOINTMENT WITH A GOOD FACIALIST TWICE A YEAR FOR PROFESSIONAL ADVICE ON PRODUCTS BEST SUITED TO YOUR SKIN.

NIAMH BRETT, WATERFORD

> 'BEAUTY IS BEING DIFFERENT. I AM BEAUTIFUL BECAUSE I TRY TO DRESS AND ACT LIKE ME AND NOT ACT LIKE EVERYONE ELSE. I LOVE TO DRESS DIFFERENTLY: I AM OPEN TO NEW IDEAS.'

› DON'T TAKE ADVICE FROM ACROSS THE MAKE-UP COUNTER — ENSURE YOUR SKIN IS CLEANSED AND EXAMINED AT CLOSE QUARTERS IN ALL ITS NAKED GLORY!

› DON'T RUSH INTO BUYING A FULL SET OF SKINCARE PRODUCTS. I RECOMMEND STARTING WITH A CLEANSER AND ASK FOR A FEW SAMPLES OF MOISTURISER TO ENSURE THE PRODUCTS WORK FOR YOU.

› DON'T MIX PRODUCTS FROM A WIDE RANGE OF BRANDS. PRODUCTS WITHIN A SKINCARE LINE ARE DESIGNED TO COMPLEMENT EACH OTHER.

› LOOK FOR PRODUCTS CONTAINING HIGH CONCENTRATIONS OF NATURAL ACTIVE INGREDIENTS. DON'T TAKE THE SALES ASSISTANT'S WORD FOR IT — ASK FOR THE PERCENTAGE OF ACTIVE INGREDIENTS CONTAINED IN EACH PRODUCT.

CLEANSING

Daily cleansing is the foundation of good skin. While often neglected, cleansing the skin day and night is the most important step in your daily programme. Irrespective of skin type, always choose a cream cleanser and rinse with plenty of warm water. The primary ingredient in cream cleansers is oil, which will protect delicate, dehydrated skin from the drying effects of water. Meanwhile, nothing breaks down sebum in blocked pores more successfully than oil for a deep cleanse. A neutral cleansing product often recommended by dermatologists is Cetaphil.

PURIFYING AND EXFOLIATING

Traditionally, alcohol-based toners are recommended to close the pores after cleansing. Alcohol has a drying effect and can irritate sensitive skin. Instead I recommend a balancing lotion to re-establish the natural oil production in the skin, while exfoliating gently. Choose a product containing gentle AHAs, such as lactic, malic and salicylic acid to exfoliate and hydrate the skin gently on a daily basis. My star recommendation is Lotion P50 by Biologique Recherche, a cult product known as a 'facial in a bottle'.

Rachel Walsh

We all know that over-exposure to the sun is damaging, but how do we protect our skin? I recommend a combined approach:

The best form of sun protection is physical. When in the sun for extended periods, wear a hat to protect the face and clothing to protect the chest, arms and legs.

Sunscreen is the second defence against sun damage. Topical sunscreen is available as a physical and chemical sun barrier and a product containing both offers the best protection. However, the use of chemicals on a daily basis can irritate the skin. I suggest that you adapt the sunscreen you choose according to your needs on a given day: when working indoors all day with minimal exposure to sunlight, I recommend a mineral foundation containing the physical sunscreens titanium dioxide and zinc. Typically, these products are oil free and offer an SPF20 without irritating the skin. When exposed to the sun for extended periods of time, particularly in summer months and travelling south, I recommend a sunscreen with a minimum SPF30. Two brands I like are La Roche Posay and the once-a-day formula by Ultrasun.

A diet high in antioxidants has been shown in studies to protect the DNA of skin cells from damage caused by UVA and UVB light. Superstar foods to protect your skin include blueberries and raspberries, green tea, tomatoes and dark leafy vegetables, in addition to foods high in Vitamin C, E and the mineral selenium.

TOP TIPS FOR BEAUTIFUL SKIN

> AS A GENERAL RULE OF THUMB, AND IN PARTICULAR IF YOU SUFFER FROM ANY BLEMISHES, REDUCE YOUR INTAKE OF PROCESSED FOOD, DAIRY PRODUCTS AND SUGAR. ACNE AND ACNE ROSACEA SUFFERERS SHOULD ESPECIALLY AVOID SPICY FOOD AND ALCOHOL AS BOTH INCREASE INFLAMMATION OF THE SKIN.

> THE SKIN IS THE LARGEST ORGAN OF ELIMINATION. IF YOUR SKIN IS CONGESTED IT'S IMPORTANT TO ENSURE THAT YOUR DIGESTION IS WORKING EFFICIENTLY. YOU CAN DO THIS BY INCORPORATING ENOUGH FIBRE INTO YOUR DIET EVERY DAY.

> ONE POTENT AND SIMPLE WAY TO PERFECT SKIN IS TO DRINK ONE 8-OZ GLASS OF ORGANIC CARROT JUICE EVERY DAY. CARROT JUICE IS RICH IN ANTIOXIDANTS, INCLUDING PHYTO-CHEMICALS, VITAMINS AND MINERALS, WHICH PROTECT, NOURISH AND MOISTURISE THE SKIN. CARROT JUICE IS PARTICULARLY EFFECTIVE IN TREATING BLEMISHES AND ACNE.

> INCREASE YOUR INTAKE OF OILY FISH TO BOOST LEVELS OF OMEGAS 3 AND 6, TO SMOOTH SKIN AND TO BANISH WRINKLES.

> FOR CLEAR, BRIGHT EYES, DRINK AN INFUSION OF GOJI BERRIES (ONE TABLESPOON) WITH CHRYSANTHEMUM-FLOWER TEA (YOU'LL FIND IT IN ASIAN FOOD SHOPS).

PROFESSIONAL HELP

Professional treatments are a valuable tool in treating skin problems and maintaining muscle definition. I recommend a facial treatment every 4–8 weeks, depending on age. However, ensure that the facial you receive is a treatment you could not have performed yourself. Avoid paying to have a therapist simply apply and remove a mask. Use the money instead to buy a mask and apply at home!

A good facial should always:

> BEGIN WITH A THOROUGH SKIN ANALYSIS

> INCORPORATE SPECIALISED EXFOLIATION AND PURIFYING TECHNIQUES

> CALM AND HYDRATE THE SKIN

> ENHANCE MUSCLE TONE AND DEFINITION, WHILE STIMULATING THE CIRCULATION OF BLOOD TO THE SKIN

> LOOK OUT FOR MUSCULAR STIMULATION TECHNIQUES INCORPORATING HIGH AND MEDIUM ELECTRICAL FREQUENCY

> MESO-THERAPY IS A USEFUL TECHNIQUE TO NATURALLY SIMULATE COLLAGEN AND ELASTIN FIBROBLASTS TO PLUMP OUT WRINKLES AND SMOOTH THE COMPLEXION

#YOURBESTYOU

WHEN ASKED TO RECOMMEND ONE FACIAL TREATMENT ABOVE ALL OTHERS, I CHOOSE COSMETIC ACUPUNCTURE EVERY TIME. COSMETIC ACUPUNCTURE ENHANCES FACIAL MUSCLE TONE AND SOFTENS WRINKLES WHILE REBALANCING THE BODY TO TREAT COMMON HEALTH CONDITIONS. THE EFFECTS OF COSMETIC ACUPUNCTURE LAST FAR BEYOND THE COURSE OF TREATMENT.

MAKE-UP MADE EASY

Both of us are very keen on the magic properties of make-up. Genetics and care can take you so far but why not reach for the fairy dust to make you look like, well, *Your Best You!* We've worked with some of the world's best make-up artists and their wealth of knowledge and tips still leave us agog. Who better than globe-trotting make-up artist **CHRISTINE LUCIGNANO** to share her insights and insider trading!

I have been painting the faces of women for more than 25 years. All types, young, not so young, make-up lovers, make-up phobes, light-skinned, dark-skinned and every skin tone in between. Women are my canvas and I have learned a lot about this living, breathing canvas! One thing is for certain, make-up can enhance your look and your mood. If your budget is tight or you can't fit into your favorite jeans, make-up never fails to pick you up again. You can always buy a new lipstick or a new eyeshadow palette and *voilà*, you have got your quick fashion fix without breaking the bank or worrying about what size you're wearing!

SKIN FIRST

It is a fact that if you look after your skin, it shows. And if you don't, the opposite is true. Yes, genes, diet and age will affect your skin, but from what I've observed, the number one most important factor is care. Even if you're a lover of the outdoors or some of the evils we humans partake in, such as alcohol, cigarettes and stress, you can help to improve the overall look of your skin.

Here are a few things we ALL need in our make-up diet:

ENVIRONMENTAL PROTECTION. During all of mother nature's seasons, whether you live in a sunny country or a cloud-covered country, if you spend time indoors or outdoors, you all need to include a certain level of protection. Protection from pollution, street dirt, UVA, UVB and UVC rays, free radicals, wind,

Christine Lucignano

ROISIN DONNELLAN, DUBLIN

'BEAUTY IS ON THE INSIDE RATHER THAN THE OUTSIDE. LOOKS ARE ONE THING, BUT IT'S WHEN YOU GET TO KNOW SOMEONE'S INNER BEAUTY, YOU FIND THE MAGIC. I AM CREATIVE MUSICALLY AND IN THE ARTS. I HAVE UNUSUAL FEATURES. BUT I TRY TO MAKE SOMEONE'S DAY EVERY DAY.'

cold, heat and sunlight. Every reputable cosmetic company, from 'mass' to 'prestige' (i.e. budget to bank-breaking), offers products that will protect you from all of these day-to-day risks. Technology being what it is and moving at the rate it does, environmental protection is attainable and affordable for all.

EXFOLIATE, EXFOLIATE, EXFOLIATE. Such an important step to any good skin. Obviously one size does not fit all so you must consider your skin type, any skin conditions, your health or any medications you might be taking before deciding on an exfoliation regime. For me, a little science is so important when choosing exfoliation products, to tame mother nature. The idea of using a product with, say, ground apricot kernels is one that I don't relish. All one has to do is look at the skin under a magnifying device and you will see the actual lacerations that you receive from repeated use of nature without the addition of science. Another example is fruit acids. It's a great idea to use fermented grape-seeds on skin because the natural acids will help to reveal a fresher, refined skin, but add the science to it and the good bits are harnessed, while the not so good bits are eliminated.

HYDRATION. Whether you are dry or oily, you must *hydrate* your skin. It is a fact that oily skin or skin with acne is almost always dehydrated. Science tells us that it is often because the skin is thirsty that it overcompensates with its own oil output. It is our job to balance this with moisturisers/serums/moisture masks that are designed for each skin type. If your skin is oily, then seek out a moisturizer that is oil free. *This will not make you more oily*, but the opposite: it will keep you hydrated, while toning down your skin's production of oil. If your skin is dry, moisturise with a product that is a bit richer, that may contain some oils. Nature's oils are usually lighter in weight and can be found in shea, jojoba, algae, olives, rosehip, etc. . . . If your skin is oily, you should also look for products that are 'oil controlling'. Oil-controlling products usually have ingredients that will help control the shine through the day and keep the skin clearer of the micro-sized germs and organisims that add to an oily-skinned girl's issues!

KEEP THE SKIN CLEAN AND FED! Typically, the skin looks for its nourishment at night as the skin is not only nocturnal but it is a living organ, unlike hair or nails. So, clean skin before bed is crucial as well as is some evening hydration. Don't forget about the fragile eye and lip area when hydrating. As there are no natural oils being produced on your lips and no pores around your eyes, these two areas will need specific products that are targeted to *deliver* and *maintain* moisture. This means a wax-stick product is ineffective for the lips, as there is nothing being delivered to the lips, so there is nothing to maintain.

#YOURBESTYOU

REMEMBER, YOU DON'T HAVE TO 'SQUEAK' AFTER CLEANSING TO BE CLEAN!

FOUNDATIONS, TINTS, CONCEALERS AND POWDERS

It's simple, less is more here! *Foundation* was not and is not designed to change the colour of your skin or take away your freckles or deny your ethnicity. Foundations (of any coverage or finish) are designed to even out your skin tone. This means, in a nutshell, to correct redness, dullness or lack of luminosity, and to conceal spots, scars and uneven texture. This is why it is crucial to own both a foundation product and a concealing product. So, if you have spots around your chin, you pin-point conceal — you don't need to apply heavy coverage to the entire face. Luminous, even and blemish free is the goal.

Powder is used generally to do two things, to finish/set your application of wet products, i.e. moisturiser, foundation, tint, etc and secondly, to blot out that shine that appears sometimes after your foundation has been applied. Powder comes in the form of a compact and is best to blot onto the skin. Generally, this is a step that is very important for camera work and depending on your skin type/conditions, it is a personal preference for every other instance.

Powders now are so technologically advanced that your skin finish actually looks/feels much better when you use a finishing powder. My preference is a loose formula for this crucial step and I use it for all skins, from dry to oily, but in a different way.

FACE SHAPE

Face shape is so individual and make-up can help you to either celebrate this, intensify it or to do a little bit of subtle correcting work. The use of *contour* and *highlighting* products are the most

#YOURBESTYOU

DON'T FORGET TO USE A GOOD BLUSHER. APPLY TO THE APPLES OF THE CHEEKS AS A GENERAL RULE AND LESS IS MORE IN THE BEGINNING. YOU CAN ALWAYS APPLY A BIT MORE, BUT DO IT IN LEVELS AS IT IS EASIER TO ADD THAN TO SUBTRACT. I PERSONALLY LOVE CREAM BLUSH FORMULAS AS IT GIVES THE LOOK OF NATURAL BLUSH WITHOUT LOOKING CAKED OR FAKE.

effective way to influence your face shape. If you want to make an area recede or look deeper, then you use the principle of 'contour', using a highlight directly above the area that has been contoured or shaped. This will instantly contrast and give more of a result. If you want to bring out an area of the face like the chin or the tip of the nose or even make a forehead appear to look bigger, then you should lighten that area. This is generally done with a highlighting product. I would caution not to have too much shimmer or metallic in your highlighter, as this will really make the area or feature protrude and if you are in daylight, it will appear even more so.

It takes a bit of practice, but mastering your own face shape and enhancing or playing down certain aspects of it can be one of the most effective things in make-up.

EYE MAKE-UP

Eyeshadows, pencils, liquid/gel/cream eyeliners, brow powders/pencils/gels, mascara . . . all of these can be used to affect two crucial aspects of your eyes: the *shape* and the *colour*. So the products you use and the way you apply them are everything. These products should not be chosen to go with your outfit or your skin tone.

Your eye shape comes from genes/ethnicity as well as your age. Depending on your application of eye make-up, you can make an eye appear more round or more almond in shape. You can make an eye look smaller or bigger and you can make an eye appear more lifted or youthful. You can even make an eye look more or less deep set. Eye shape changes as we get older, so our application needs to change, whereas your eye colour stays basically the same. So colours that suit you at 20 generally suit you at 70. It's really the application that needs to evolve over time!

There are literally hunderds of variables when it comes to eye shape and it's not easy to give hard-and-fast rules, but there are some basic principles:

› APPLYING LIGHT COLOUR TO AN AREA OF THE EYE WILL BRING IT OUT OR MAKE IT LOOK BIGGER. APPLYING DARK COLOUR TO AN AREA WILL MAKE THE AREA LOOK SMALLER AND OFTEN STRONGER.

> APPLYING PRODUCTS WITH A SLIGHT UPWARD ANGLE WILL HELP TO DEFY GRAVITY OR GIVE A BIT MORE OF A YOUTHFUL APPEARANCE.

> APPLYING DARKER SHADOWS TO A SAGGING OR HEAVY EYE AREA, IF DONE VERY SUBTLY AND BLENDED VERY WELL, CAN 'LIFT OUT' THAT HEAVY APPEARANCE.

The colour of your eye is very much influenced by the colours that surround it. Some eyes actually appear to change colour when a certain shade is worn next to them. I believe that using colour theory is crucial to getting the most out of your eye colour.

Blue eyes with white or grey flecks appear bluer when you use colours that are cooler in the undertone. So reach for a brown that looks more silvery or taupe in colour or any version of grey, as well as certain blues/burgundies/plums or mauves.

Blue eyes with yellow/gold/rust flecks appear more intense when you use colours that are warmer in the undertone. Look for browns that are more cinnamon, rusty, golden. Think of spices, earthy tones and metals (especially gold, bronze and copper).

Green eyes usually come one of two versions: solid green (from light to dark) or colour flecked (with golds, hazels, green and sometimes even white). To get more contrast or intensity out of solid green, many of the browns with a mustard shade as well as many greens from mint, khaki, olive to forest green will do the trick. This eye tone is also quite receptive to purples or plum-based colours. Be careful though, as the colours you use on your eye are meant to contrast, which will showcase your eye colour, but if you go too far in one direction, you could see the eyeshadow first and not your own eye colour. Use the shadows to your advantage! For green eyes with flecks, use the same rule of thumb, but add accent colours that are similar to your fleck colours and you will see some interesting changes. For example, a green-eyed girl with yellow flecks can pick up a yellow-to-gold colour and place it around the eye in a form of pencil, colour pop under brow, etc.

Brown is the most versatile of eye colours. The basic rule of thumb is to try and activate the flecks in a brown eye. So if you see any colour flecks like rust, yellow, green or white, then use those shades to accent. This will ultimately make your eye colour

ALI O'CALLAGHAN, CORK

'MY IDEA OF BEAUTY IS CONFIDENCE AND BEING COMFORTABLE IN YOUR OWN SKIN. MY HAIR IS MY BEST FEATURE.'

appear more multi-dimentional and interesting. If you have a solid or a dark-brown-to-black eye, then usually using a contrast such as a metallic influence or a lighter shade next to the iris will give you more interest. The only colour family I am careful with when it comes to a brown-eyed girl is purple, as it can make you look tired or unwell if you aren't careful.

LIPS

The most sensual area on a woman's face by far is her lips. When lips are dry or cracked or lacking pigment, this is the quickest way to look lacklustre. On the other hand, the lips are the one feature that you can enhance/change the quickest. A few rules:

Close your mouth while you line or shape your lips. You will have a better chance of perfecting your lip shape if you simply close and relax your mouth.

Always fill in your lip first with your liner or your base lip product *before* you attempt to change your shape or add fullness. And if you are adding fullness with either a pencil or a gloss or a lighter shade than the base, do this in the centre of the lip either top, bottom or both. Trust me, if you want it to look believable, then don't add fullness to the *outer* area of the lips, top or bottom.

To make lips appear naturally fuller, err on the side of a lighter shade or a shade that has a bit of pearl or a metallic feel. Matte shades are usually not what you're looking for as they tend to make a lip look smaller and more one dimensional.

EVERYONE can wear a red! That's right, ladies, everyone can and should have a red that suits them. The smaller your lips, the more sheer and/or bright your choice should be. And remember that reds generally fall into one of two colour families: *cool* or *warm*. So to really generalise, this means that lighter-skinned girls look more subtle in a cool red, whereas a darker-skinned girl looks more subtle in a warm red. But you really have to venture out and try many different reds to find the ones that you like best. The only constant is that the warmer/yellower the red, the yellower your teeth can appear! So make sure you look at your smile after applying as you may need to add a bit of cool in the undertone to enhance your tooth colour.

Always *hydrate*. No lips look good when they are dry or dull. Even if you don't like wearing lipstick, your lips look much better if you keep them hydrated. Using a product at night before bed is crucial, as is the use of a balm (that delivers and maintains moisture) during the day. For ladies who love their lipstick, make sure you not only hydrate at night but again before applying your lipstick and search out lipsticks with hydrating formulas.

A FEW FINAL THOUGHTS. . .

> ALL COSMETICS HAVE A SHELF LIFE, SO BE WISE AND DON'T HOLD ONTO A PRODUCT FOR TOO LONG. DRY OR POWDER PRODUCTS ARE GENERALLY OK FOR A LONGER PERIOD, WHEREAS ANYTHING MOIST OR WET USUALLY 'GOES OFF' QUICKER. OLD MASCARA IS THE BIG NO-NO WHEN IT COMES TO MAKE-UP. A SEALED, DARK AND WET PLACE IS WHERE MASCARA LIVES AND YOU DON'T WANT TO RISK YOUR EYE BECOMING ANGRY FROM A MASCARA THAT HAS GONE OFF!

> TOOLS ARE THE UNSEEN HEROS OF MAKEUP. GOOD, CLEAN BRUSHES AS WELL AS LASH-CURLERS, TWEEZERS, SPONGES, ETC. ARE INVALUABLE. KEEP THEM CLEAN AND YOU MAY HAVE THEM FOR YEARS. OBVIOUSLY, WHEN IT COMES TO SPONGES OR LASH-CURLERS, THERE ARE SHELF-LIFE/MAINTAINANCE ISSUES, SO MAKE SURE YOU ASK YOUR COSMETIC SPECIALIST WHEN BUYING THESE PRODUCTS!

> GET A GOOD FACIAL EVERY TIME THE SEASON CHANGES.

> HAVE A MAKE-UP LESSON FROM A PRO SO YOU CAN CUSTOMIZE AND OPTIMIZE YOUR MAKE-UP APPLICATION.

> NATURAL DAYLIGHT OR AS CLOSE TO IT AS POSSIBLE IS THE BEST LIGHT IN WHICH TO APPLY YOUR MAKE-UP. IF YOU LIKE YOUR MAKE-UP IN THIS LIGHT, THEN YOU WILL LIKE IT IN ANY LIGHT.

> NOW, GET STUCK IN, GIRLS, AND HAVE A PLAY WITH MAKE-UP. IT'S YOUR FRIEND AND IS THERE TO HELP YOU LOOK AND FEEL BETTER!

GORGEOUS HAIR

Now that you have healthy, glowing skin, let's take a look at hair care. We asked one of our favourite hair messers, **ZARA COX**, to give us some pearls of wisdom to inspire you to look after those locks.

- -

I've spent the last twenty years building my experience in the craft of hairdressing and my love of all things hair, which has culminated in opening Queen (www.queen.ie). I think that your hair is often a barometer of all the things going on in your life, from the stresses of modern living to major life changes, like having babies. It's so very important to us, but not the highest on your body's list of things to take care of, so sometimes it needs extra TLC. Here are a few tips on how to get the hair you want:

FIRST, NUTRIENTS

The foundation for new, healthy hair is the nutrients we consume. Hair that is fed with good nutrients will not break or thin as easily. As we all know, plenty of sleep, the right food and drinking water are the best ingredients for healthy locks, however, given our hectic lifestyles, this is not always easy. Our hair texture changes at different ages and stages of our lives, which really affects the growth and health of your hair. Puberty, pregnancy, menopause, medication, illness, hormonal changes, dieting and stress can all have a major impact on your hair. Including good fish oils in your diet and taking vitamin supplements that are specifically designed for hair can really make a difference. Ask your stylist to talk you through the things you can change: shape, colour and using products to make your hair look its best, no matter what stage of life you're at.

#YOURBESTYOU

CARE TIPS FOR EVERYONE

BRUSH YOUR HAIR *BEFORE* WASHING AS IT'S MORE FRAGILE WHEN WET

SLEEP ON A SATIN OR SILK PILLOWCASE — LESS BED-HEAD AND FEWER WRINKLES

PROTECT FROM HEAT: STYLING TOOLS CAN REALLY DAMAGE HAIR

USE SUN PROTECTION: IT STOPS COLOUR FADE AND PROTECTS HAIR

DON'T ROUGHLY TOWEL-DRY HAIR. BLOT INSTEAD: IT CAUSES LESS BREAKAGE

SPEND MORE TIME MASSAGING HAIR WHEN SHAMPOOING: IT'S GREAT FOR A HEALTHY SCALP

Zara Cox

CLEANSE, CONDITION AND TREAT

I am a self-confessed product junkie and I really believe in the power of products, but I also believe you need the right products for you rather than a press full of bad-hair days. Choosing the right products can be bewildering; choosing the wrong ones a waste of time and money. Ask your stylist to analyse your hair and scalp and your hair's specific needs. The right shampoo and conditioner can dramatically change the appearance of your hair and make your life a whole lot easier. We all need a treat sometimes and your hair is no different.

WHAT HAIRCUT SUITS MY FACE SHAPE?

There is not only one haircut to suit any individual — it's all about creating a frame for your face, highlighting your best features and downplaying the bits you don't love so much. But certain haircuts suit certain face shapes. If your face is . . .

ROUND. . .

TRY: Fullness and height at the crown, long hair, centre partings, side fringes, and short hair.
AVOID: Bobs, too much volume at the sides, side partings, heavy fringes, chin-length haircuts, width and *very* short hair.

SQUARE. . .

TRY: Layers and movement, height at the crown, grown-out fringes, side partings, and texture around the face, textured fringes and volume.
AVOID: Jaw-length haircuts, centre partings, very flat styles, square shapes, straight-across fringes and too-short hair.

OVAL...

TRY: Can wear most hairstyles and lengths, so hair texture is most important, hair looks great off the face.

AVOID: Heavy fringes, too much hair on face.

RECTANGLE...

TRY: Graduations, shorter, textured haircuts with volume, layered styles, texturised fringes, side fringes, straight fringes, side partings. Width at sides, fullness is good.

AVOID: Too much length around face, too much height, especially at fringe/crown, flat hair, and centre-partings.

HEART...

TRY: Side fringes, side partings, height on top with longer looks, chin-length styles.

AVOID: Straight blunt fringes, width at sides, top-heavy looks, short graduation, and square mid-lengths.

PEAR/TRIANGLE...

TRY: Volume, layered haircuts, side partings, bring attention to the forehead.

AVOID: Heavy fringes, chin-length haircuts, width around sides. Triangle is a pear shape, so don't create more width in the wrong area.

DIAMOND. . .

TRY: Width at sides or jaw-length cut, tuck hair behind the ears, side partings, and blunt fringes.

AVOID: Centre partings, too-short hair or too much height on top.

OTHER THINGS TO CONSIDER:

› DO YOU NORMALLY WEAR GLASSES? IF SO, BRING THEM WITH YOU.
› CERTAIN CUTS MAY SUIT YOUR FACE SHAPE, BUT NOT YOUR HAIR TEXTURE OR GROWTH PATTERNS.

TEXTURE

The relationship between your hair type and texture will definitely affect the type of hairstyle you can have. What are your needs? Do you want to wash and go, or does your lifestyle require a more polished look. The further you stray from your natural texture, the higher the maintenance will be. This is definitely one to discuss with your stylist. It is possible to change your texture with different treatments, products, techniques and hair tools, all of which will require a commitment of time. Ask your stylist for tips and tricks so you can get the same result at home.

COLOURING

Natural tone, colour history and the condition of the hair are the most important things to consider when colouring your hair. If you have a lot of colour build-up in your hair, it's important to give both yourself and your hairdresser time to achieve your desired look.

Nothing is impossible when it comes to colouring your hair; some things just take a long time. The condition of your hair is always extremely important. If the natural colour of your hair is black, then going blonde will require a lot of maintenance, which means

#YOURBESTYOU

GETTING THE RIGHT HAIRCUT . . .

FIRSTLY, YOU NEED THE RIGHT HAIRDRESSER. RECOMMENDATIONS ARE BEST, SO ASK AROUND.

DON'T BE AFRAID TO STOP PEOPLE IN THE STREET IF THEY HAVE A GOOD HAIRCUT; IT'S ALWAYS A GREAT COMPLIMENT TO THEM.

CONSULTATION IS KEY, SO DO YOUR HOMEWORK. STYLISTS LOVE PICTURES, THEY LITERALLY TELL A THOUSAND WORDS.

A GOOD HAIRDRESSER WILL TELL YOU IF YOUR EXPECTATIONS ARE REALISTIC FOR YOUR HAIR. TELL THEM HOW MUCH TIME AND EFFORT YOU HAVE TO PUT INTO YOUR HAIR. YOUR HAIRCUT HAS GOT TO WORK WITH YOUR LIFESTYLE.

EIMEAR DE SOUZA, DROGHEDA

'BEAUTY IS UNIQUENESS, HEALTH SHINING THROUGH LAUGHTER AND A SMILE AND LOVE IN YOUR EYES. I AM BEAUTIFUL BECAUSE I MAKE DIFFERENT CHOICES AND HAVE LEARNED NOT TO BE ASHAMED OF THIS, BUT TO BE PROUD INSTEAD! I'VE HAD LOTS OF SURGERIES AND HAVE SEVERAL SCARS FROM THOSE ON MY BODY. TO ME, EACH ONE IS A MEDAL, A REMINDER TO BE PROUD OF WHAT I'VE COME THROUGH.'

a lot of damage, so it's not always the best option. There is no point in having the colour you want if it means your hair is going to be in bad condition. It will never look good.

Venturing too far away from your natural colour is not always a good idea. Your natural depth is always going to suit you. More than likely, it just needs to be enhanced. If you have a lot of natural red in your hair it might just be a matter of working with what you already have rather than against it. This will generally give you the best results. Home care is also very important. Using the right products to keep your colour looking healthy and shiny is half the battle.

STYLING ▶

Remember, your hair can be really fun. Your lifestyle may dictate your everyday look, but we all need to let our hair down sometimes. Don't be afraid to try something new – it's only temporary and can be changed back with a little shampoo. Different tools, from crimpers to wands, can add a little magic to your look. Invest in the right tools and brushes and, most importantly, products; these are the easiest way to dramatically change your hair. Just go for it!

WELL-BEING:
THE POWER OF INNER BEAUTY

HEALTH AND FITNESS PLAYS AN ENORMOUS PART IN BOTH OUR LIVES, BECAUSE WE KNOW THAT IT DIRECTLY IMPACTS ON HOW YOU LOOK. IT'S MUCH EASIER TO LOOK YOUR BEST IF YOU FEEL GREAT, AND STUDIES SHOW THAT PHYSICAL FITNESS CAN HAVE A GREAT IMPACT IN BOOSTING MENTAL HEALTH, TOO. WHICH IS WHY WE'VE DEVOTED THIS CHAPTER TO YOUR WELL-BEING, INVITING TWO OF IRELAND'S BEST-KNOWN HEALTH GURUS, KARL HENRY, OF KARL HENRY FITNESS AND *OPERATION TRANSFORMATION*, AND FITNESS AND DANCE PROFESSIONAL JANE SHORTALL, TO TALK

ABOUT THE IMPORTANCE OF EXERCISE. AND, IF YOU WANT TO KEEP YOUR SKIN IN TIP-TOP CONDITION, NUTRITIONAL THERAPIST ANDREA CULLEN HAS PUT TOGETHER A SEVEN-DAY PLAN FOR HEALTHIER SKIN.

KARL HENRY'S ESSENTIAL TIPS ON HEALTH AND FITNESS

Looking good on the outside is important to so many of us, but your body's well-being is of equal importance. Life has become so stressful that we place our bodies under an immense amount of pressure, and if you don't take care of yourself, then eventually your body will break down. We all know the benefits of exercise, but here are some easy tips to improve your well-being. Anyone can use them! For further information see www.karlhenry.ie.

EAT REGULAR MEALS

Eating meals throughout the day will help keep your metabolism stable as well as burning calories all day long. When we don't eat for an extended amount of time, it actually slows down the body, reducing your natural calorie-burning abilities. There is a great debate about whether it's better to eat three or five meals a day: I tend to use three meals and two snacks as a guide. Breakfast is the most important meal: it kick-starts your body for the day, so no matter what happens, don't skip it! Your snacks can consist of fruit

Karl Henry

or small meals, full of nutrients. No matter what way you choose to eat, you must keep your diet low in sugar and starch; these two foods are not only bad for your waistline, they are bad for your health!

GIVE YOUR STOMACH TIME TO CATCH UP

After we've eaten, it takes our bodies ten to fifteen minutes to realise we've had enough to eat. Because of this delay in feeling full, it is very easy to eat more than our bodies actually need, leaving us with that Christmas day overfull sensation. Then your body will tell you it needs sleep, because it's using all its energy to digest the food! So, you need to begin chewing your food and slowing down your eating, leaving your knife and fork down between each chew.

EAT WHOLE FRESH FOODS

In order for foods to last as long as they do on shelves in the supermarkets, they are filled with preservatives, which in turn deplete the nutrients and vitamins originally found in those foods. When possible, purchase fresh foods and avoid pre-packaged and convenient fast food, as these types of food are typically higher in calories, fat and salt, as well as preservatives. If you have local markets in your area, why not pick up your fruit and veg there? You will get fresher produce and you will be supporting the local economy, too.

GET MOVING

Our bodies were not meant to sit behind a desk all day long. We need daily exercise to benefit our overall health and especially to strengthen all our muscles, including our heart. Exercise can also help you sleep better and improve your mood, so whether it's a high-impact workout at the gym or a stroll through the neighbourhood, hit the pavement and get moving! You should be getting in at least thirty minutes every day as a minimum guideline.

BE A DETECTIVE WITH FOOD LABELS

When reading the list of ingredients on packaged foods, if you do not recognise the ingredient or can't pronounce it, perhaps this isn't something you want to put in your body. If you see a product with a huge list of ingredients, put the item right back on the shelf. You really want to look at the sugar content; if it's high (i.e. 40% or more of the carbohydrate content) put it back on the shelf and find another variant!

EAT YOUR WHOLEGRAINS

Wholegrains are unrefined products that have maintained their nutrients and fibre content, unlike white products, which are left with no nutritional value. An additional benefit to eating 100% wholegrains, such as breads and pastas, is that they help maintain blood sugar levels, with less spiking and crashing throughout the day. Wholegrains also keep you fuller for longer.

EAT THE 'RIGHT' FAT

Fat has a reputation for being bad for us and in many cases this is true. Overeating the wrong fats (saturated fats) can lead to gaining those unwanted pounds as well as increasing your risk of heart disease. However, there are healthy fats that our bodies actually need. Stick to healthy fat sources that are unsaturated, such as olive oil instead of butter or margarine, which contain saturated fat. Good fats are essential for body functions, so don't avoid them!

Jane Shortall

With these simple rules in mind, you can begin to think about health and fitness. **JANE SHORTALL** of Jane Shortall Dance (www.janeshortall.com), who has introduced the concept of dance fitness to Ireland, talks about feeling good through exercise.

THE FEEL-GOOD FACTOR IN HEALTH AND WELL-BEING

#YOURBESTYOU
WHEN YOUR HEALTH IS GOOD, YOU WILL FEEL GOOD ABOUT YOU!

The best way for you to start feeling great and looking fabulous is by exercising more and eating less. I know that this is easier said than done, but imagine yourself looking and feeling beautiful in your favourite outfit — you can make this happen by simply making some changes to your lifestyle. By improving your diet and including exercise in your daily routine, not only will you look fabulous, you will feel much better in mind, body and spirit.

Exercise should not be considered a chore in your daily routine. You should feel excited when starting out on this 'health and well-being' programme. Try to think of it as a challenge to improve yourself in the most fun way possible. Close your eyes and visualise a 'fit and slim' you, someone who looks and feels amazing and who has an abundance of energy and a positive zest for life. You will probably start feeling motivated just thinking about this!

Many of us find that the most difficult part of exercise is self-motivation and then 'sticking to it'. The excuses to avoid exercise are endless: 'I have no time', 'I'm too tired', 'It's too cold outside', 'I should be working on the laptop instead'. But instead of tiring you out, exercise actually does the reverse and revitalises and energises you. When you exercise, you are more productive. Exercise not only helps you burn fat, lose inches and tone muscle, it also decreases stress and increases self-esteem.

The endorphins will kick in and make you feel instantly happy, confident and capable.

For me, being healthy and well has many benefits:

> TACKLING DIFFICULT TASKS OR ISSUES IS SO MUCH EASIER WHEN YOU ARE HEALTHY AND WELL.

> YOU CAN ACCOMPLISH SO MUCH MORE IN YOUR LIFE WHEN YOU ARE HEALTHY AND WELL.

> THE QUALITY OF YOUR LIFE AND THE RELATIONSHIP YOU HAVE WITH YOURSELF, FAMILY AND FRIENDS WILL IMPROVE WHEN YOU ARE HEALTHY AND WELL.

> YOU CAN FIGHT OFF ILLNESS AND DISEASE MORE SUCCESSFULLY WHEN YOU ARE HEALTHY AND WELL.

> YOU CAN GIVE YOURSELF THE CHOICE OF ENJOYING A LONG, FULFILLING, MEANINGFUL LIFE WHEN YOU TAKE STEPS TO BECOMING HEALTHY AND WELL TODAY.

MAKING EXERCISE FUN

Here are some of my tips to help you make positive changes to maintaining a healthier lifestyle, which ultimately will make you feel and look AMAZING!

- *The most important thing to do when starting out an exercise programme is to choose an activity that you enjoy. Try to exercise with friends and make exercise a fun experience (cycle, hike, walk, swim, dance or play any sport you enjoy).*

- *Ten minutes is better than no minutes each day, but try to exercise at least three times a week, preferably for one hour.*

- *Motivate yourself to exercise (this is the difficult bit). Try to play music while you are preparing to leave the house: this will help you get in the mood. Always wear comfortable, loose clothing with the correct footwear when you exercise. When you look the part, you act the part and you will find that it helps you to work to your full potential when you exercise.*

- If you can't leave the house to exercise, play music and dance at home or dance while you are doing the housework and cooking. Not only will it help you to start losing inches, it will de-stress your mind and enhance your spirit. There is a wide choice of dance and exercise DVDs on the market today that would be suitable and safe for you to follow at home.

- Once you have started an exercise plan, you will see and feel results in no time and you will be hooked! The 'feel-good' result from all your hard work is so addictive that you will want that same feeling forever more, but it is important to choose a fun activity and make it varied to avoid repetition. It will also work different muscle groups and help you reach your fitness goals faster.

STAYING MOTIVATED

Don't give up on exercise once you find that you fit into your favourite old jeans or a new dress. If you do that, you will slip straight back into your old habits. Remember, exercise is about a lifestyle change so CHOOSE AN ACTIVITY THAT YOU ENJOY.

- You will not sustain an exercise plan if you do not like it. Exercise must be enjoyable and give you a feeling of accomplishment. As soon as you start to see and feel improvement, you will feel motivated to continue.

- You will have setbacks, but don't be hard on yourself; you are still making progress and every day will not be your best one, so don't be discouraged.

- Let your body recover and renew itself by getting adequate sleep. It is important to try and get at least seven to eight hours' sleep a night. Sleep boosts your immune system. Sleep gives your body time to rest, recover and rejuvenate.

- **Always consult a doctor when starting out an exercise programme, particularly if you are over 50 years old and have not exercised in a long time, or if you have a history of illness.**

- Begin slowly and build up activity gradually over a period of months. It should not feel overwhelming, so don't overdo it at the beginning. It will also help if you take it easy when you start exercise so that you avoid muscle soreness and injury.

- Try to carry out 30 minutes of moderate-intensity activity each day.

NUTRITION: SEVEN DAYS TO FABULOUS SKIN

If a fish in dirty water was sluggish and sickly, would you drop in a tablet or change the water?

Of course, you'd change the water. The adage, 'You are what you eat' has been around for a very long time but if you're feeling low in energy or are in a cycle of self-criticism, a kick-start for your system could be just what you need. We've both tried this nutritional plan, developed by nutritional therapist **ANDREA CULLEN** of AC Health Solutions (www.achealthesolutions.com), to give you fabulous skin. Not only will it do what it says on the tin, the associated benefits are boundless energy and a great sense of well-being. We urge you to give it a go: you won't be disappointed.

SEVEN DAYS TO FABULOUS SKIN

What we eat (and what we don't eat) has a profound effect on our health and skin vitality. The first step towards beautiful, radiant skin should be from the inside. The food and beverages we consume provide the ingredients to form and nourish our skin. The health of our skin today reflects our diet, lifestyle, and health in recent months. The health of our skin, hair and nails and our energy and vitality in the coming weeks is all down to how we eat, breathe, sleep, and move today.

I believe that when a woman eats well and takes care of her body, it places her back in control and helps her to feel proud of her body. There is nothing sexier than a woman who is glowing from the inside out, who is fit and healthy and exuding confidence. When we meet a woman with glowing skin, we never fail to notice and comment on it, but beautiful skin is something

Andrea Cullen

NIAMH CASEY, KILDARE

'I AM BEAUTIFUL BECAUSE I EMBRACE WHO I AM, I WEAR MULTI-COLOURED NAILS AND PLATINUM BLONDE HAIR WITH EITHER PINK OR PURPLE. I DON'T KNOW IF THAT'S CLASSED AS BEAUTIFUL IN THE TYPICAL SENSE, BUT IT MAKES ME FEEL LIKE ME.'

that each and all of us can afford and achieve without expensive potions or spa retreats.

Over the years, I have developed my own diet and nutrition programme for skin, which adds my own insight and practical tips to the latest research in the areas of skin health and anti-ageing. This programme is based on many years of my own research in developing diets for health and fighting illness, as well as from my work with chronic health conditions. My background as a pharmacist has also given me experience dealing with common troublesome skin conditions.

This condensed, fast-track seven-day plan for skin health does not require the use of nutritional supplements. It's perfect for implementing in the week prior to an important event, holiday or wedding. Too many women punish themselves with overly strict and restrictive diets before important events, not realising that although the number on the scales may drop, so, too, may the vitality of their skin. This seven-day plan will not only help you drop a few pounds, but it will bring clarity, vitality and lift to your skin.

Many factors influence the health and appearance of skin tissue and the ageing process:

> SUN DAMAGE AND POOR SKIN CARE

> GENETIC TENDENCY

> POOR DIET AND DEFICIENCIES OF PROTEIN, ESSENTIAL FATTY ACIDS AND ANTIOXIDANTS, MINERALS AND VITAMINS

> STRESS

> HORMONE IMBALANCE

> ENVIRONMENTAL STRESS, E.G., SMOKING, CHEMICAL EXPOSURE, PROCESSED FOOD, MEDICATIONS, ETC.

> GASTROINTESTINAL HEALTH — DIGESTIVE FUNCTION AND THE BALANCE OF BENEFICIAL MICROBES IN THE GUT PLAY AN IMPORTANT ROLE IN THE HEALTH OF OUR SKIN

> DETOXIFICATION FUNCTION — THE SKIN IS THE FINAL ROUTE OF ELIMINATION IN THE DETOXIFICATION PROCESS AND OVERBURDENED LIVER, KIDNEYS AND GASTROINTESTINAL SYSTEMS MAY LEAD TO SKIN PROBLEMS

> POOR BOWEL FUNCTION

Experts have long recognised that diet and nutrients in the body play a key role in skin health. While other organ systems may demonstrate a capacity to withstand nutritional negligence, the skin cannot, and usually manifests the negative effects of nutritional deficiencies within a relatively short period of time. Every one of us can relate to this: skin outbreaks after a period of stress, lack of exercise or poor diet sound familiar? Puffy skin after a night out or too many take-aways? Rapid ageing as witnessed in the chronic dieters or smokers in our circle of friends? The more we neglect our health, the more difficult it becomes to undo the negative effects on our skin.

What about the person who eats well, takes regular exercise and takes care of themselves and has fabulous radiant dewy skin? This isn't just genes! Individuals who maintain a better overall nutritional status (through better diet and the use of supplements) over their lifetimes typically show less skin ageing than those with a nutritionally inferior diet and a lack of supplementation.

Optimal support of the skin requires a wide range of nutritional materials that are not always readily available in the typical standard diet, and so a nutrient-packed diet as recommended here is required to boost skin health. The most common nutrition mistake I see amongst women coming to see me complaining of poor health and lacklustre skin is a diet lacking in quality protein and healthy fats, and most are a long way shy of the recommended six portions of vegetables daily. *If I ask you to do one favour for your health, then it is to switch from being the calorie-counting police to becoming the nutritional-density detective.* Instead of focusing on deprivation, become creative and inventive in power-packing your diet with healing nutrients.

It has been only very recently and due to advances in science that we have been able to understand how to properly support the skin with nutritional supplements designed to provide long-term health benefits. I suggest, however, that you start with a diet overhaul before you consider adding specialist supplements. *Adding supplements to an inferior quality diet is akin to not cleansing your face yet applying expensive face creams: it simply doesn't make sense!* Improving your diet will have a far more profound effect than most of us realise.

Without veering into non-nutritional territory, I am also going to add here that how you breathe and move also beneficially influences your skin. While following this plan, I recommend that you exercise regularly. Walking, yoga, Pilates, weight training and cardio training most days is recommended, in addition to getting outdoors. Skin-brushing, deep-tissue or lymphatic massage, deep breathing and aiming for at least seven to eight hours' sleep at night is also encouraged. Sleeping on your back is recommended as sleeping on your face has been shown to increase wrinkling (and also neck problems). If you suffer from constipation, consider adding in a source of fibre to this plan, such as Psyllium husks, aloe vera, or specialist fibre products. These should be taken in the evening with a large glass of water before bed. And if you smoke, then for your own sake, quit. I recommend that you do so with the support of a professional.

Our skin is a true mirror of our health, and it is important for us to start deciphering the message that our skin is telling us when its health is not optimal.

SEVEN DAYS TO FABULOUS SKIN — THE PLAN

DAYS 1 TO 5

ON WAKING: LEMON DRINK WITH GINGER

1 CUP OF BOILED WATER

JUICE OF $\frac{1}{2}$ TO 1 LEMON

PINCH OF CAYENNE RED PEPPER

SEVERAL PINCHES OF GROUND CINNAMON

1–2 TEASPOONS OF FINELY GRATED GINGER

Mix the lemon juice, cayenne pepper, ground cinnamon and ginger in a large mug. Add boiling water to the mixture, while stirring. Drink hot or allow to cool before drinking.

The cayenne pepper stimulates the body's metabolism, the lemon juice stimulates the digestive and liver systems, whilst also alkalinising the body, and the ginger contains powerful anti-inflammatory compounds. This drink is a fabulous wake-up call to your body first thing in the morning (or at any point during your day).

***•QUICK TIP:** push the ginger through a garlic press and make sure to catch the ginger juice as it has a habit of squirting everywhere. I also add the squashed ginger bit from the garlic press back into my cup to prevent wasting any goodness.*

•If you do not like cayenne pepper, then consider adding some chopped sprigs of fresh rosemary, a wonderful herb to wake you up while also providing antioxidant and anti-inflammatory compounds.

BREAKFAST: AN HOUR LATER APPROXIMATELY

4–6 OZ / 110–170G GRILLED, STEAMED OR POACHED FRESH WILD OR
  ORGANIC SALMON

AND/OR 2 POACHED EGGS

AND/OR SMALL PORTION OF COOKED PORRIDGE, MULTIGRAIN
  'PORRIDGE'(SEE OVERLEAF), OR COOKED WHOLEGRAIN CEREAL MADE
  WITH FILTERED WATER OR NON-DAIRY MILK

*To this, add 2 tablespoons of whole soaked flaxseeds and serve
with your choice of non-dairy milk.*

*Sweeten your 'porridge' with ground cinnamon, nutmeg or mixed
spice and if preferred serve with unsweetened coconut flakes and
your chosen fruit or berries.*

2-INCH WEDGE OF CANTALOUPE OR WATERMELON

OR $^1/_3$ CUP FRESH BERRIES

*No juice, coffee, regular breakfast cereal, or toast. If you normally
drink large amounts of coffee, drink black or green tea to prevent
caffeine withdrawal.*

8–12 OZ/225–350 ML FILTERED WATER OR GREEN TEA

*•This is a large breakfast, you have the option of alternating the
salmon, eggs or cooked porridge options. Enjoy the flaxseeds and
fruit daily.*

BEST BREAKFAST GRAINS: GLUTEN-FREE PORRIDGE OATS

Multi-grain 'porridge': choose one, two, or a blend of the following: gluten-free oatmeal or porridge flakes, brown rice flakes, buckwheat flakes, millet flakes, or quinoa flakes. Simply mix and cook as you would porridge. Soaking the grains overnight in water or non-dairy milk speeds cooking time and may prove helpful if you are in a hurry in the morning.

COOKED WHOLEGRAINS

- BROWN RICE · MILLET · BUCKWHEAT/KASHA
- WHOLE ROLLED OATS

You may prepare a batch of one or a mixture of the above wholegrains in advance for several days. Store in the fridge and each morning reheat your required portion and serve as directed. The above grains all have a similar cooking time of approximately 45 to 50 minutes.

BEST FRUITS:

- Berries — blueberries, blackberries, raspberries, loganberries, strawberries, black and red currants

- Cherries

- Pomegranate — I recommend at least one if not two servings daily; add variety into your regime with the occasional substitution of the other fruits suggested here: Melon — watermelon, melon and cantaloupe (the more coloured the flesh, the better)

- Low-sugar, nutrient-dense fruits: fresh apricots, deeply coloured plums, kiwi, and papaya

MORNING SNACK

GREEN TEA OR HEALTHY TEA BLEND

(Recommended teas include green, nettle, horsetail, milk thistle, peppermint, fennel, dandelion leaf or root, or detox tea blends. The lemon ginger drink or lemon rosemary drink are also recommended.)

6 WALNUT OR PECAN HALVES

OR 1–2 HEAPED TEASPOONS ORGANIC ALMOND, PUMPKIN SEED OR
   HAZELNUT BUTTER

OR 2 SMALL SQUARES HIGH-COCOA-CONTENT ORGANIC DARK
   CHOCOLATE

If you wish to power up your nutrition, then add a fresh juice made in a juicer using the following ingredients: fresh kale, watercress, rocket, or a mixture of these leaves (juice sufficient leaves to make enough juice to fill half a small tumbler), unwaxed lemon (skin, pith and all; seeds removed), washed pear or apple.

LUNCH

4–6 OZ/ 110–170G FRESH ORGANIC/WILD SALMON (GRILLED, BAKED,
   STEAMED, OR POACHED)

QUICK OPTION: *canned Alaskan wild or sockeye salmon or wild Atlantic salmon. Serve plain or as suggested in recipe section. Add 1 tbsp chopped fresh herbs (e.g. parsley, coriander, basil, or dill).*

2 CUPS GREEN SALAD DRESSED WITH HOME-MADE DRESSING

OR 2 CUPS FRESH STEAMED GREENS

Toss the steamed greens in 1 teaspoon of extra virgin coconut oil/olive oil. To add flavour sprinkle with dried cumin, crushed fresh garlic, fresh or dried herbs, dried ground turmeric, or other recommended seasonings.

FRUIT: *optional if you are still hungry: pomegranate, 1 kiwi fruit, or portion of cantaloupe or berries.*

8–12 OZ / 225–350 ML FILTERED WATER OR GREEN TEA.

AISLING GUEST, TIPPERARY

'I THINK I'M BEAUTIFUL BECAUSE I AM A NICE PERSON WITH A LOVELY SMILE, NICE EYES, FABULOUS EYELASHES, GOOD BOOBS AND A NICE BUM! MY HUSBAND NOMINATED ME.'

BEST SALAD GREENS

Watercress

Rocket

Red chard

Dark green or green/purple lettuce

Chicory (red, purple or green)
Radicchio

Whole organic spinach leaves

Fresh coriander leaves

Fresh herbs/dandelion

Chinese cabbage

Buk choy/pak choy

Purslane

RECOMMENDED VEGETABLES

TO CHOP OR GRATE INTO YOUR SALAD
FOR FLAVOUR AND TEXTURE:

Fennel

Red onion

Green scallions

Broccoli

Red cabbage

Fresh sprouts

Cucumber

Carrots

Red, yellow, orange and green peppers

Celery

Snow peas

Baby asparagus

Radishes

Left-over steamed vegetables

BEST GREENS FOR STEAMING

I.E. ANYTHING DARK GREEN AND LEAFY!

Leafy cabbage

Seasonal leafy greens

Kale

Broccoli/purple broccoli

Leeks

Spinach

Brussels sprouts

Broccoli shoots

Buk choy

Asparagus

Pak choy

Purple or Chinese cabbage

Swiss chard

Courgettes

Green beans

Snap peas

Mange tout

Red cabbage

SKIN-BOOSTING HERBS AND SPICES

TO ADD TO YOUR LUNCH, DINNER, AND SALAD DRESSINGS FOR BONUS BENEFITS:

Garlic

Ginger

Turmeric

Fennel seeds

Fresh coriander

Chilli

Cayenne pepper

Chives

Oregano

Rosemary

Thyme

Dill

Black pepper

Paprika

Parsley

Cumin

Curry spices

Thai spices

Garam masala mix

Ground fenugreek

PERMITTED CONDIMENTS FOR SEASONING

Extra virgin cold pressed oils
(coconut, olive, flax, hemp, mixed blends)

Fresh / dried herbs

Dijon mustard

Seasoning spice mix

Black pepper

Lemon or lime juice

Small dash of Himalayan or Celtic sea salt

MID-AFTERNOON SNACK

Choose one of:

1 small cup chopped vegetables such as snow peas, raw baby asparagus, baby beans, colourful peppers, celery, carrots or 1 cup of home-made soup.

+ 4 large king-size prawns or 2 oz / 50g slice of turkey/chicken breast served with a dash of good quality pesto, tapenade or tomato salsa (preferably home-made or low in added sugar) or 1 tablespoon home made guacamole or mashed avocado or home-made hummus.

OR

Small carton plain (unsweetened) yoghurt or Greek yoghurt + generous dash of cinnamon.

+/- 1 apple or pear (washed, skin on).

+/- Small handful of nuts: hazelnuts, walnuts, pecans, Brazil nuts, or almonds OR 2 teaspoons pumpkin or sunflower seeds.

+/- 1 teaspoon almond nut butter or tahini paste stirred through the yoghurt.

DINNER

Same as lunch.

BEFORE BEDTIME SNACK

Choose a small portion of one of suggested afternoon snack options, if hungry.

WEEKEND MENU PLANS FOR DAYS SIX AND SEVEN

WEEKEND BREAKFAST

After your morning lemon and ginger drink, whisk up a power shake.

POWER SHAKE

1 SERVING OF VEGETARIAN PROTEIN POWDER (APPROX 12G TO 15G PROTEIN SERVING)

NON-DAIRY MILK TO DESIRED CONSISTENCY

$^{1}/_{2}$ CUP FROZEN OR FRESH WASHED BERRIES

SMALL BUNCH OF KALE, SPINACH, ROCKET, OR WATERCRESS (START WITH A FEW LEAVES AND ADD ACCORDING TO TASTE)

SERVING OF ACAI CONCENTRATE OR POWDER (I LIKE NOW ACAI LIQUID CONCENTRATE)

2 TABLESPOONS CHIA OR FLAX SEEDS (PREFERABLY GROUND; IF WHOLE BLEND YOUR SMOOTHIE WELL)

$^{1}/_{2}$ TO 1 TEASPOON CINNAMON POWDER

Option to add unsweetened coconut flakes (healthy fats).

•Blend well in the blender; add a few ice cubes if you would like to thicken this up if you are using fresh berries.

WEEKEND LUNCH

Poached or boiled egg or duck egg, served with 50g smoked wild or organic salmon, wilted or steamed spinach and chopped $^{1}/_{3}$ avocado.

2 cups green salad dressed with dash of balsamic vinegar or balsamic vinegar syrup.

WEEKEND SNACK

As an added option to the above you may choose a sliced apple or pear served with a few small squares of high-cocoa-content organic dark chocolate or 2 teaspoons of organic almond nut butter.

WEEKEND DINNER

Chicken curry served on brown rice or quinoa with steamed greens (aim to keep your vegetable portion large and your rice or quinoa portion small), or grilled chicken (may be marinated in spices or herbs) served with selection of roasted vegetables and a side portion of steamed baby potatoes (I recommend adding a dash of sea salt and a generous sprinkling of freshly chopped or dried rosemary).

OPTIONAL DESSERT

Baked or stewed apples or pears with berries served with Greek or natural unsweetened yoghurt. Option to sweeten with ground cinnamon, mixed spices, Stevia, Lo-Han, or Xylitol.

HELPFUL TIPS

- Aim to eat at least two servings of salmon daily; the greater your intake of omega 3, DMAE, calcitonin, vitamin D, astaxanthin and fish protein from salmon, the better!

- I recommend that you buy salmon from the fishmonger and when possible, choose wild or Irish organically-farmed-at-sea salmon, as this is better quality, more nutrient-dense and lower in pollutants than farmed salmon. Your fishmonger will be able to advise you on the best selection. It may save you time to buy and cook in bulk. Store uncooked fish in the freezer and cooked fish in well-sealed containers in the fridge. Several cutlets or fillets of salmon may be prepared in advance. Steaming, poaching, grilling or baking are healthy cooking methods and herbs and spices may be used to add flavour.

- When possible eat the skin (scales removed) or the flesh right under the skin (the deep-brown coloured meat) as this is especially nutritious and rich in peptides and oils. However, should you be cooking farmed non-organic salmon, then I suggest that you remove the skin as this has been shown to contain measurable amounts of persistent organic pollutants (POPs) when salmon swim in contaminated waters.

- If you get fed up with salmon, then trout is an option. Crab, prawn and lobster are alternatives that are rich in astaxanthin, although less rich in omega 3; mackerel and haddock are also rich in omega 3, but not as beneficial as salmon while on this plan. Do your best to eat as much salmon as possible for optimal skin benefits.

- The best way to cook salmon is by using methods that will keep it moist and tender. Salmon can be easily overcooked and become dry, so be sure to watch your cooking times. Poaching or steaming salmon results in very moist flesh; another option is to bake the salmon covered with a few centimetres of filtered water in the base of the dish or aluminium foil. Extra care should be taken when grilling, as burning can damage nutrients and create free radicals that can be harmful to your health.

- I do not recommend smoked salmon for this skin plan, due to its nitrate and salt content, except on the weekend days to provide variety. It may, however, be chosen on occasion if you are pressed for time. Choose *wild or organic smoked salmon* when possible. Smoked wild salmon is the superior choice and can often be found in Dunnes Stores, sometimes for half price.

- Buy the best quality fruit, vegetables, fish and poultry that you can. This means organic, wild, caught- or farmed-at-sea, free-range and/or local when at all possible. Wash produce well with filtered water, veggie wash or Kangen pH 11.5 water.

- A word on water. Water is the substance of life, every chemical reaction in our body must occur in water, and for optimal health, cellular hydration is crucial. Our skin glows when we are optimally hydrated. I recommend Kangen water, an electrically ionised alkaline, highly antioxidant, micro-clustered water. More information is available at www.kwdemo.com. Water at the very least should be filtered and when possible should not be purchased in plastic bottles. Instead, carry your filtered water in a BPA-free or stainless-steel container. These are widely available online or in sports or adventure stores.

- Aim to vary the suggested vegetables and fruits over the seven days … Variety is the secret to achieving optimal intake of key nutrients that are important for the skin.

- This plan is gluten free, with only a very limited intake of gluten-free grains when indicated. If you notice a dramatic improvement to your overall health or significant weight loss, then it may be worth consulting a nutritional therapist specialising in gluten intolerance to see whether you have an intolerance to gluten-containing foods.

- Make six portions of vegetables (at least) your daily goal.

- Apart from natural unsweetened organic yoghurt or Greek yoghurt, no dairy is recommended on this plan. Recommended delicious options include nut or almond milk, Kara coconut milk, quinoa, hemp, or rice milk. I do not recommend that soya milk is used as a milk substitute. Similarly, oat milk contains gluten and so is omitted from this plan.

- Recommended vegetarian protein powder options include brown rice protein, hemp protein, pea protein, and sprouted grain protein blends. My favourite brands include Jarrow formulas, Garden of Life, Vega Sequel Naturals, Pure encapsulations, Sun Warrior, and Pulsin. These are available online, in good health stores, or from achealthdirect@eircom.net.

- Superb websites for ordering health foods, should they not be available in the stores, include: www.goodnessdirect.co.uk and www.iherb.com.

- Whole soaked flax seeds are recommended as part of breakfast on this plan. Simply soak two tablespoons of flaxseeds overnight in a small tumbler of water, with the water approximately 1 inch over the seeds.

- Nut butters are simply a form of peanut butter made from healthier nuts. Tasty options include almond, walnut, Brazil nut or pecan nut butters. Pumpkinseed butter is also available and is incredibly nutritious.

- Breakfast 'porridge' may be prepared using water or non-dairy milk. I suggest soaking your grains overnight to speed the cooking time. Once your 'porridge' is prepared, add your soaked flax seeds, sweetening of choice and, should you prefer, fruit and unsweetened coconut flakes.

- If sweetening or flavouring is needed on your breakfast 'porridge', add sweet spices such as ground cinnamon or mixed spice, dried natural coconut flakes or a pinch of salt. Sugar is not recommended. Stevia, Xylitol, or Lo-Han are healthy sweeteners with no calorific value or unwanted health effects. Aspartame is not recommended (EVER).

- Limit salt. Use this opportunity to break your salt habit. However, if you train or exercise intensely every day or have low blood pressure or extreme fatigue, then some lo-salt, Himalayan sea salt or Celtic salt is permitted.

- Salads should be dressed with a small amount of oil to aid the absorption of fat-soluble nutrients and antioxidants.

- To add taste to vegetables, I recommend tossing in extra-virgin organic oils and the recommended herbs or spices.

- If you work away from home, bring pre-prepared snacks and meals with you.

- Some delicate leafy greens such as chard, asparagus, kale, and spinach cook in only a few minutes, while others such as leeks and sprouts take up to five minutes or more. This means steaming separately or adding the faster-cooking leaves later. Over-cooking will reduce the nutritional content of the vegetables and affect their taste.

- Sea-weeds are found in most health stores. I personally like wakame, hijiki and kombu and highly recommend their inclusion in your skin programme.

SELECTED RECIPES

DRESSINGS FOR YOUR SALAD OR VEGETABLES

When choosing olive oil, choose the best that you can afford. Good-quality olive oil is extra virgin, cold pressed and taken from the first pressing.

You may alter your use of olive oil with other healthful oil blends such as flax oil, hemp oil, evening primrose oil, oil blends such as Omega Nutrition Essential Balance Oil or Barleans the Essential Woman Oil. Choose high-quality oils that are cold pressed and store in the fridge.

OLIVE OIL, BALSAMIC VINEGAR AND DIJON MUSTARD DRESSING

This dressing is my tried-and-trusted dressing and due to the way I cook when speed is of the essence, never gets measured out accurately. I simply take the following ingredients in the suggested approximate amounts and shake well in a glass jar. This dressing lasts when stored in the fridge. Shake well before use.

EXTRA VIRGIN OLIVE OIL OR A MIXED BLEND OF COLD PRESSED OILS

BALSAMIC VINEGAR

(APPROXIMATELY TWO PARTS OIL TO ONE PART VINEGAR)

2 TBSP (APPROXIMATELY) DIJON MUSTARD

1–2 TSP IRISH HONEY

GENEROUS AMOUNT OF FRESHLY GROUND BLACK PEPPER

OPTIONAL FRESH OR DRIED HERBS SUCH AS ROSEMARY, OREGANO, PARSLEY OR CORIANDER.

BLENDED LEMON-OIL DRESSING WITH GARLIC

1 CUP EXTRA VIRGIN OLIVE OIL OR A MIXED BLEND OF
   COLD PRESSED OILS

2–4 TBSP LEMON JUICE

2–3 CLOVES GARLIC, MINCED/CRUSHED/ FINELY CHOPPED
   (OMIT THE GARLIC IF YOU ARE SENSITIVE TO GARLIC)

1 CUP FRESH PARSLEY — CHOPPED

$1/2$ TSP SEA SALT

SEVERAL DASHES CAYENNE RED PEPPER

OPTIONAL (RECOMMENDED): $1/2$ TSP OF ONE OR MORE OF THE
   FOLLOWING: OREGANO, BASIL AND/OR CORIANDER

Mix together all the ingredients in a jam jar and shake well. Refrigerate for a couple of hours so the herbs and flavours can mingle. Serve chilled or at room temperature on salads.

Don't be afraid to add additional spices and herbs to these dressings to further improve their skin benefits.

POWER SOUP RECIPE

Makes about 8 cups or 2 litres.

The soup is a filling snack that will boost your nutrition and re-alkalinise your system — perfect for glowing skin. This soup may be eaten as it is or blended in a blender or using a hand held blender, should you prefer a smoother soup. Extra portions may be frozen or stored in the fridge for later consumption.

The following recipe can be varied according to taste or availability of produce. Feel free to mix, match, and vary the vegetables to create your own variation of the soup, however, it is recommended that root vegetables are avoided while on this programme apart from the two carrots recommended here for sweetening. I recommend chopping the vegetables as small as you can if you are not blending the soup.

For every 3 litres of filtered water add:

1 large chopped onion

1 large chopped leek

2 cloves or more of garlic, finely chopped (aged smoked garlic adds great flavour)

2 sliced carrots

1 diced courgette

2 cups of chopped greens: kale, parsley, spinach, chard, coriander, Chinese cabbage, pak choi, or other greens (as many different dark greens as possible)

2 celery stalks

· cup of seaweed: nori, dulse, wakame, kelp, or kombu (recommended, chop or tear before washing)

· cup of cabbage (preferably a dark green or curly variety)

2 inch piece of fresh ginger, peeled and finely chopped

Sea salt to taste (in moderation)

If available, add 1 cup of fresh or dried shitake or maitake mushrooms (these have powerful immune-boosting properties)

Sauté the onions, leeks and garlic in extra virgin olive oil or virgin coconut oil in a large saucepan or soup pot until starting to soften. Then add all the remaining ingredients (filtered water also) and simmer for approximately 60 minutes.

Serve the soup as it is or cool and blend to desired consistency. Store in a large, tightly sealed glass container or Tupperware in the fridge, removing small portions and reheating for your snacks or meals. Extra portions may be frozen.

This delicious soup may be enjoyed for your morning or afternoon snacks. It is important to complement it with your chosen serving of protein: prawns, chicken or turkey (which may be stirred through the soup if preferred).

DIP RECIPES

HUMMUS SPREAD

1 CUP DRY CHICK PEAS — SOAKED OVERNIGHT, RINSED WELL AND
  COOKED (RINSING SEVERAL TIMES) OR USE TINNED CHICK PEAS
  IF TIME LIMITED (KEEP THE JUICE FROM THE TIN FOR ALTERING
  CONSISTENCY OF THE SPREAD)

1–2 TBSP SESAME TAHINI

2–3 TSP FRESH ONION — GRATED OR CHOPPED VERY FINELY

2 CLOVES GARLIC — CRUSHED

2–3 TSP GLUTEN-FREE SOYA SAUCE

2 TSP CUMIN SEEDS OR POWDER

1 TBSP FRESH CHOPPED PARSLEY

$^1/_2$ –1 TSP SEA SALT

$^1/_2$ –1 TSP EACH: OREGANO AND CELERY SEED

$^1/_2$ –1 TSP EACH GROUND CORIANDER AND GROUND CLOVES

$^1/_2$ –1 TSP OR MORE CAYENNE RED PEPPER TO TASTE

*Cook the chick peas until tender, then drain and save the liquid.
While the chick peas are still hot, mash them together with the
onion and all the rest of the ingredients (if using canned beans,
there is no need to heat the beans). Herbs and spices may be
altered according to personal taste. (Extra liquid from cooking the
beans/saved from the tinned beans may be added to the mixture
if it is too dry. Leftover spread may be refrigerated for up to 7
days.*

PUY LENTIL HUMMUS

175G PUY LENTILS (ALSO KNOWN AS DARK GREEN SPECKLED LENTILS),
  RINSED AND DRAINED

1 RIPE AVOCADO

2 TBSP CHOPPED PARSLEY OR CORIANDER

1 TBSP LEMON JUICE

1 GARLIC CLOVE (OPTIONAL)

Cover the lentils with 500ml cold water in a saucepan and bring to the boil. Simmer gently for about 30 minutes, stirring occasionally until the liquid has been absorbed. Allow to cool. Transfer to a blender and add the garlic clove (if liked), the avocado, parsley or coriander and lemon juice. Blend to a rough purée, adding a little water if necessary, and season to taste with salt and pepper.

I usually add some spices to this, such as chipotle pepper or garam masala, as I like my dips to have a kick. A spicier dip also means that you tend to use the dip more sparingly.

GUACAMOLE

1 LARGE RIPE AVOCADO — PEELED AND MASHED

1 TSP ONION — CRUSHED OR VERY FINELY CHOPPED OR POWDER

$^1/_2$ TSP PAPRIKA

SEVERAL PINCHES EACH: CAYENNE RED PEPPER AND CUMIN

FEW DROPS OF GLUTEN-FREE SOYA SAUCE

SALT TO TASTE

OPTIONAL: 3–4 TSP FRESH LEMON OR LIME JUICE

Mix all the ingredients together and chill half an hour before using to keep fresh. If used for a dip, bury the avocado pit in the bottom of the dip bowl to help to keep the dip fresh for longer.

SALMON RECIPES

When preparing salmon, I suggest that you prepare a few fillets each time to cut back on your time in the kitchen. Given how much salmon you will be eating while following this programme, it makes sense to make your life as simple as possible.

TO OVEN BAKE SALMON CUTLETS OR FILLETS

Baking salmon in aluminium foil or a Pyrex dish in the oven is a handy, quick method of preparation. I tend to add water under the salmon, as this creates a steaming effect when the fish is cooking, and keeps the salmon deliciously moist.

To prepare your fish, simply wash the fish and pat dry with kitchen roll. Place the prepared fish in the centre of a large piece of foil or a glass Pyrex dish, which has been brushed with extra-virgin olive or coconut oil. Season with lemon juice, sea salt and black pepper (other fresh herbs may be used such as thyme, coriander, parsley, dill, hot spice mix, turmeric, etc.).

Bring the edges of the foil around the sides of the fish and scrunch it together at either end to form a canoe-shaped parcel and then bring together and seal or, if using a Pyrex dish, simply replace the glass lid. As mentioned above, I suggest adding one to two centimetres of water to the base of the fish to improve its moisture and prevent it drying out.

Carefully lift the parcel onto a large baking sheet or place directly onto the rails of the oven and bake in a preheated oven at 220°C/425°F for 10–30 minutes depending on the size and thickness of the fish.

Remove the fish from the oven and open up the parcel. Carefully check to see if the fish is cooked by using a knife or fork, the flakes of fish will move apart easily and no longer look see-through. Avoid over-cooking the fish as the fish will continue to cook once removed from the oven. Remove from the foil and serve.

JENNIFER MURRAY, WICKLOW

'I THINK BEAUTY IS SOMEONE WHO IS CONFIDENT IN THEMSELVES AND WHO IS NOT AFRAID TO SHOW THEIR OWN STYLE AND PERSONALITY. I AM BEAUTIFUL BECAUSE I AM CONFIDENT IN MY BODY AND IN MYSELF. I LIKE TO HAVE FUN AND I AM NOT AFRAID TO BE MYSELF, MAD AND ALL AS I AM SOMETIMES!'

GRILLED SALMON

Wash the fish steaks or fillets and place in a Pyrex dish with about $1/4$–$1/3$ inch of water. Rub each piece with a dollop of extra virgin olive oil or virgin coconut oil. Add a few splashes of gluten-free Tamari /gluten-free soya sauce, a squeeze of fresh lemon/lime juice over each piece and any other herbs or seasoning of choice.

Steaks: Grill the steaks for 7–12 minutes on the first side and 3–6 minutes on the second.

Fillets: Grill the fillets for 3–7 minutes on the first side and 2–5 minutes on the second.

Serve as is or with lemon wedges and fresh chopped parsley.

TO COOK SALMON IN A STEAMER

Pour about 2.5 cm/ 1 inch of water into the bottom of a shallow pan with a well-fitting lid. Put a petal steamer (looks like a fan, is cheap to buy and available from supermarkets and cooking utensil stores) into the pan, bring the water to the boil and then lay the prepared fish on the steamer.

Sprinkle the fish with some chopped ginger if you have time (or other seasoning of choice). Cover with the lid, reduce the heat to medium and steam for 8–12 minutes or until cooked through.

Salmon may also be steamed on the top of an electric basket steamer, with your vegetables in the baskets (e.g. Tefal or Breville steamers are commonly available from most stores or Argos).

TO PREPARE CANNED SALMON

Canned (wild red Atlantic or Alaskan) salmon is especially good for your skin. The deep red pigments of these salmon are rich in Astaxanthin, an extremely powerful antioxidant with numerous benefits for our skin as well as our health. Choose the varieties that still contain the skin and bones.

Mix your drained salmon with one or a combination of the following:

Avocado dip or mashed avocado

Dijon mustard

Hummus (preferably home made)

Chopped fresh parsley, dill, or coriander

Black pepper or a dash of dried chipotle peppers or chilli peppers

Chipotle chilli sauce

Lemon or lime juice

1 tbsp low-fat natural probiotic yoghurt

BUTT RUB SALMON

This is my favourite salmon recipe as it earns a star for the inclusion of the anti-inflammatory and antioxidant spice turmeric and is very quick to prepare. The Butt rub seasoning is from the USA and can be purchased on eBay; alternatively many spicy seasoning mixes are available in the supermarkets locally, such as fish or Cajun spice mix.

Salmon fillets or cutlets

Butt rub

Turmeric powder

Dash of coconut oil

Rub the prepared salmon portions with coconut oil and season generously with Butt rub and turmeric. Cook as suggested in the oven, under the grill, or in a steamer.

WEEKEND RECIPES

FRUITY CHICKEN CURRY

If preferred, monkfish may be substituted for the chicken.
(Serves 4)

EXTRA VIRGIN OLIVE OR COCONUT OIL

1 RED ONION — CHOPPED

2 CLOVES GARLIC — CRUSHED OR FINELY CHOPPED

1 TBSP CURRY POWDER (MORE IF YOU LIKE IT HOT)

400 G CAN CHOPPED TOMATOES

125 ML/ $^1/_2$ CUP STOCK MADE FROM KALLO ORGANIC OR JUST
   BOUILLON OR OTHER MSG-FREE AND GLUTEN-FREE STOCK CUBES

FRUIT CHUTNEY (I USE BALLYMALOE RELISH; THIS IS QUITE A
   SWEET CHUTNEY, SO I RECOMMEND ADDING IT TABLESPOON BY
   TABLESPOON TO YOUR PREFERRED LEVEL OF SWEETNESS)

500G CHICKEN OR MONKFISH (OR APPROXIMATELY 3 TO 4 FILLETS) —
   CUT INTO SMALL CUBES

$^1/_2$ TO 1 CUP FRESHLY TORN CORIANDER LEAVES ADDED JUST PRIOR TO
   SERVING

4 TBSP LOW-FAT NATURAL YOGHURT, TO SERVE

*Cook the onion in a dash of oil over a medium heat for 3 minutes
or until soft. Add the garlic and curry powder and cook, stirring,
for about 30 seconds. Add the remaining ingredients (except the
coriander and yoghurt) and bring to the boil. Reduce the heat and
simmer, partially covered, for about 20 minutes or until the chicken
(or monkfish) is cooked through.*

*Serve the curry topped with a dollop of yoghurt over steamed
greens.*

ROASTED VEGETABLES

Ordinarily, roasted vegetables taste delicious when root vegetables are included; while on this plan, however, it is recommended that root vegetables are limited.

Roughly chop an assortment of vegetables such as red onions, fennel, courgettes, garlic bulbs (whole), peppers, halved tomatoes or whole pierced cherry tomatoes, asparagus, mushrooms, etc. Place on a roasting tray and splash with olive oil, sea salt, black pepper and herbs of choice (my favourite are mixed herbs, rosemary or thyme). Cook at approximately 200° to 230°C for roughly 20 minutes until cooked, turning now and again. If some vegetables appear to be cooking more quickly than others (e.g. asparagus), then remove these as the others finish cooking. Serve immediately, or serve cold.

SOME FINAL THOUGHTS

WE ARE PASSIONATE ABOUT THE POWER OF SELF-ESTEEM AND CONFIDENCE. WE KNOW THAT IT'S EASIER TO HAVE A GOOD DAY IF YOU'RE HAPPY WITH HOW YOU LOOK. WE ALSO KNOW THAT NOT EVERY DAY CAN BE BATHED IN SHINING LIGHT, SO BE GENTLE ON YOURSELF IN YOUR JOURNEY TO BECOME *YOUR BEST YOU*. WHAT'S CLEAR TO US, THOUGH, IS THAT FEELING GOOD ABOUT YOURSELF IS ADDICTIVE. IT MAY TAKE A LITTLE TIME AND INVESTMENT, AND HELP FROM US TO GET THERE, BUT ONCE YOU'RE THERE, ODD BAD HAIR DAYS ASIDE, YOU CAN FEEL GOOD ABOUT HOW YOU LOOK.

IF YOU'VE FOLLOWED OUR PLAN, YOU WILL HAVE A NEW SENSE OF WHO YOU ARE, WHAT YOU ARE, AND YOUR POSSIBILITIES TO BECOME *YOUR BEST YOU*. THIS BOOK IS BASED ON WHAT WE, AND OUR EXPERTS, KNOW THROUGH OUR EXPERIENCE WITH HUNDREDS OF WOMEN AND ALSO HOW WE LIVE OUR OWN LIVES. FOR US, HOW WE FEEL ON THE INSIDE IS INEXTRICABLY LINKED TO HOW WE FEEL ON THE OUTSIDE. BUT IT COMES DOWN TO YOUR OWN SENSE OF ENTITLEMENT. YOU WILL ONLY BEGIN TO FEEL GOOD ABOUT YOURSELF *IF* YOU BELIEVE YOU DESERVE THAT FEELING. WE BELIEVE EVERY WOMAN HAS THE ABILITY TO FEEL FABULOUS. YOU'VE READ THE BOOK, NOW FOLLOW THE PLAN AND PROJECT FORWARD TO A LIFE WHERE YOU ARE *YOUR BEST YOU*.

OUR SHOPPING GUIDE

YOU HAVE NOW GRADUATED FROM THE SCHOOL OF *YOUR BEST YOU*. NOW FOR THE FUN BIT: THROWING OUT ALL THOSE 'BARGAINS', BAGGY CAMOUFLAGE CLOTHES AND UNWORN BAD BUYS. ONCE YOU'VE CLEARED A SPACE IN YOUR WARDROBE, YOU CAN BEGIN TO IMPLEMENT ALL THE ADVICE WE'VE GIVEN YOU IN THIS BOOK. TO HELP YOU, WE'VE COMPILED A COMPREHENSIVE LISTING OF WHERE TO FIND ALL THOSE GREAT FUTURE BUYS. THIS WILL BE A LIFETIME'S WORK: DON'T RUSH IT, BUILD UP SLOWLY AS YOU GAIN CONFIDENCE IN YOUR NEW-FOUND SENSE OF *YOUR BEST YOU*. HAPPY SHOPPING!

VALUE DEPARTMENT STORES

DUNNES STORES
Nationwide,
www.dunnesstores.ie
(Facebook)

PENNEYS
Nationwide,
www.primark.co.uk
(Facebook, twitter)

FOREVER 21
Jervis Shopping Centre,
tel: 01 874 0112, (Facebook,
twitter)

MID-RANGE DEPARTMENT STORES

ARNOTTS
Henry St Dublin 1,
tel: 01 8050400,
www.arnotts.ie
(Facebook, twitter)

CLERYS
18-27 Lower O'Connell St,
Dublin 1,
tel: 01 8786000
www.clerys.ie
(Facebook)

DEBENHAMS,
Nationwide
www.debenhams.ie
(Facebook, twitter)

MARKS & SPENCER
Nationwide,
www.marksandspencer.ie
(Facebook, twitter)

HIGH-END DEPARTMENT STORES

BROWN THOMAS
Dublin, tel: 01 605 6666, Cork,
tel: 021 480 5555,
Limerick, tel: 061 417 222, Galway, tel: 091 565 254,
www.brownthomas.ie
(Facebook)

HARVEY NICHOLS
Dundrum Town Centre,
Dublin 14,
tel: 01 2910488,
www.harveynichols.com
(twitter)

HOUSE OF FRASER
Dundrum Town Centre,
Dublin 14,
tel: 01 2991400,
www.houseoffraser.co.uk
(Facebook, twitter)

CHAIN STORES

ALDO
Dublin- Blanchardstown
Centre, Dublin 15,
tel: 016467430,
Dundrum Town Centre, Dublin 14,
tel: 01 2968832,
Grafton St, Dublin 2,
tel: 01 6799338,
www.aldoshoes.com
(Facebook)

A·WEAR
Nationwide,
www.awear.com
(Facebook, twitter)

BARRATTS
Nationwide,
www.barratts.co.uk
(Facebook, twitter)

BT2
The Blanchardstown Centre,
Dublin 15,
tel: 01 860 6540,
Unit 133,
Dundrum Town Centre,
Dublin 14
tel: 01 296 8400,
28-29 Grafton St,
Dublin 2,
tel: 01 605 6747,
www.bt2.ie
(Facebook, twitter)

CINDERS SHOE HEAVEN
Dublin – Wicklow St,
tel: 01 6777491;
Co. Kildare –
Courtyard Shopping Centre,
Newbridge,
tel: 045 437750;
Galway – 16 Upper Abbeygate St,
Galway,
tel: 091 533696,
www.cinders.ie
(Facebook)

COAST
Nationwide,
www.coast-stores.com
(Facebook, twitter)
Dorothy Perkins
Nationwide
www.dorothyperkins.com
(Facebook, twitter)

EVANS
Nationwide,
www.evans.co.uk
(Facebook, twitter)

FRAN & JANE
Nationwide,
www.franandjane.com
(Facebook)

FRENCH CONNECTION
Nationwide
www.frenchconnection.com
(Facebook, twitter)

H&M
Nationwide
www.hm.com
(Facebook, twitter)

KAREN MILLEN
Nationwide
www.karenmillen.com
(Facebook, twitter)

MISS SELFRIDGE
Nationwide
www.missselfridge.com
(Facebook, twitter)

MONSOON
Nationwide
www.monsoon.co.uk
(Facebook, twitter)

NEW LOOK
Nationwide
www.newlook.com
(Facebook, twitter)

NEXT
Nationwide
www.nextdirect.com

OASIS
Nationwide
www.oasis-stores.com
(Facebook, twitter)

OFFICE
Nationwide
www.office.co.uk
(Facebook, twitter)

PAMELA SCOTT
Nationwide
www.pamelascott.ie
(Facebook)

REISS
Dublin – Arnotts,
BT2, 1 St Stephen's Green,
Dublin 2, tel: 01 6712588;
Kildare – Unit 30,

Kildare Village,
tel: 045 535033,
www.reissonline.com
(Facebook, twitter)

RIVER ISLAND
Nationwide
www.riverisland.com
(Facebook, twitter)

SCHUH
Nationwide
www.schuh.co.uk
(Facebook, twitter)

TED BAKER
Nationwide www.tedbaker.com
(Facebook, twitter)

TEMPTED
Sze 16-28.Dublin – Raheny,
Dublin 5, tel: 831 4293;
Wexford – Key West Shopping
Centre, Wexford,
tel: 053 9174910;
Carlow – Carlow Shopping
Centre, tel: 059 9164961,
www.tempted.ie (Facebook)

TOPSHOP
Nationwide
www.topshop.com
(Facebook, twitter)

**UNITED COLOURS OF
BENETTON**
Nationwide,
www.benetton.com
(Facebook, twitter)

WALLIS
Nationwide
www.wallis.co.uk
(Facebook, twitter)

WAREHOUSE
Nationwide
www.warehouse.co.uk
(Facebook, twitter)

ZARA
Nationwide
www.zara.com (Facebook)

KEY

(8-18) *etc refers to dress sizes available.*

 new contemporary

 accessories

 shoes

 vintage

 plus size

 lifestyle

 maternity

 occasion

 underwear

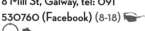 *casual*

hire

bridal

REGIONAL STORES CONNACHT

COBBLERS SHOES
Dunkellian St, Loughrea, Co. Galway, tel: 091 870244

COBWEBS
7 Quay Lane, Galway, tel: 091 564388 www.cobwebs.ie (Facebook)
Top Labels: Jewellery by Cartier, Isabelle Fa, Masriera, Rodney Rayner, Van Cleef & Arpels

COLETTE LATCHFORD
Lyndon Court, Galway, tel: 091 563630,
Top Labels: Avoca Anthology, Fenn Wright Manson, Gerard Darel, Marc Cain

DON'T CALL ME DEAR
8 Mill St, Galway, tel: 091 530760 (Facebook) (8-18)
Top Labels: Marc Jacobs, Anya Hindmarch, Philip Treacy, DVF, Joanne Hynes

DESIGN PLATFORM
The Courtyard, Clifden Station House, Connemara, Co. Galway, tel: 095 21526, www.designplatform.ie (8-18)
Top Labels: Louise Della, Sarah Pacini, Sita Murt, Annette Gortz, Lillith.

DUBARRY SHOES
Glentaun, Ballinasloe, Co. Galway, tel: 090 964 2348, www.dubarry.com, (Facebook, Twitter)
Top Labels: Shoes by Dubarry, Marine, Freedom, Country Wear, Direction and Dubes

LA FEMME
29 O'Connell St, Sligo, tel: 071 914 3331 (Facebook) (10-16)
Top Five Labels: Arruba, Betty Barclay, Didier Parakian, Evalinka, Gerry Weber

LES JUMELLES
11 Upper Abbeygate St, Galway, Tel: 091 564540, (Facebook) (10-16)
Top Labels: Kristensen du Nord, Marithé + François Girbaud, Rick Owens, Shoes by Terry de Havilland

LIBERTIES
The Quay, Westport, Co. Mayo, Tel: 098 50273 (8-18)
Top Labels: Betty Jackson, Ines Raspoort, Mary Grant, Orla Kiely, Sarah Pacini

GERRY MCGUIRE'S SHOES
Ellison St, Castlebar, Co. Mayo, Tel: 094 902 8999; Tone St, Ballina, Co. Mayo, Tel: 096 21363; www.mcguireshoes.com (Facebook) (2-8)
Top Labels: DKNY, Guess, Just Cavalli, Luciano Padovan, Ugg, Juicy Couture

GOSSAMER GIRL
Mount St, Claremorris, Co. Mayo, tel: 094 937 7783; www.gossamergirl.com (Facebook) (8-18)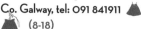
Top Labels: Jax, Meg, House of Lykke, Onstage,

MONET
30 Main St, Loughrea, Co. Galway, tel: 091 841911 (8-18)
Top Labels: Aideen Bodkin, CoCoMenthe, Miguel de Luna, Sandwich, Stills

MYRIAM O'REILLY
7 Eyre St, Galway, Tel: 091
561866 www.myriamoreilly.com,
(Facebook) 🧥 (6-18)
Top Labels: by Malene Birger,
Indies, Louise Della, Odd Molly,
Tara Jarmon, Isabel de Pedro

BORN CLOTHING
Newtownsmith, Co. Galway,
tel: 091 895224, (Facebook),
👓 (6-28) 🧥
Labels: Lipsy, Vero Moda, Jack &
Jones, Vila

PREMOLI
William St, Galway,
tel: 091 566087,
An exclusive range of leather
footwear and handbags from Italy
and Spain.

REGIS
9 Lower Abbeygate St, Galway, tel:
091 569696, (10-14) 🧥 ⃝
Labels: Aideen Bodkin, by Groth,
Critical Mass, N&C Kilkenny,
Laga

ROCOCO
Cross St, Galway, tel:091 565856,
www.rococoonline.ie, Facebook
(8-16) 👓 🧥
Labels: Noa Noa, Hoss Intropia,
Just In Case, by Tel, Mo, Rundholz

SELECT
2-3 Lismoyle House, St Augustine
St, Galway, tel: 091 532629, www.
selectboutique.ie, Facebook
(10-16) 🧥 🧥 ⃝
Labels: Almost Famous, Just B,
James Lakeland

**SERENA BOUTIQUE
NATIONWIDE**
Superquinn Shopping Centre,
Carlow Town, tel: 059 914 3360,
http://serenaboutiques.com, (8-18)
👓 🧥 👞 ⃝
Labels: Airfield, Elisa Cavaletti,
Lauren Bidal, Mais il est où le
Soleil?

SUGARPINK
The Green Room, 10 Pearse
Road, Sligo, tel: 071 915 0950,
Facebook (8-16) ⃝ 🧥
Labels: Fenn Wright Manson,
Hoss Intropia, InWear, Nougat,
Still

ZODI
8 Wine St, Sligo, tel: 071 914
5555, (3-8) ⃝
Labels: Shoes by Hispanitas,
Khrio, KMB, Luciano, Menbur and
Sachelle

ZULU
Wine St, Sligo, tel: 071 914 4738,
Facebook (8-18) 🧥 🧥 ⃝
Labels: Isabelle de Pedro, Save
The Queen, Diva, Lauren Vidal,
Sistes

DUBLIN

UCCA
15 The Westbury Mall, Dublin 2,
tel: 01 677 6321, www.ucca.ie,
Facebook (6-14) 👓 🧥 🧥
Labels: Super Fine, Bash, American Vintage, Forte

ALILA
41 Drury St, Dublin 2, tel: 01 679
9547; www.alila.ie, Facebook (8-16)
👞 🧥 ⃝
Labels: Betsey Johnson, Tony
Bowls, Miriam Ocariz. Shoes by
Suecomma, Bonnie

HONEY & RUBY
4 Johnson's Place, Dublin 2, tel: 01
677 3430, Facebook
Labels: Allicano, Honey and Ruby,
Hunter and Gatherers, Meemilied,
Clara Couture

ANASTASIA
114 Main St, Ranelagh, Dublin 6,
tel: 01 491 2037, www.anastasia.ie,
Facebook, (8-16) 🧥 👓

Labels: Anonymous by Ross +
Bute, Catherine Malandrino, Orla
Kiely, She's So, Transit

ASHLEY REEVES
Stillorgan Shopping Centre, Co.
Dublin, tel: 01 288 6276; Rathfarn-
ham Centre, Dublin 14, tel: 01 493
4609 (10-22) 🧥 🧥
Labels: Balser, Bianca, Not Your
Daughter's Jeans, Gerry Weber,
Olsen

ATELIER 27
27 Drury St, Dublin 2, tel: 01
6791211, (Facebook) (8-14) 👓
⃝
Labels: Tokiki, Jaime McEleney
Millinery, De Loup, Aliquo

AUDREY TAYLOR
Killiney View Albert Road, Sandy-
cove, tel: 01 284 1988, (10-20) 👜
⃝ 👞
Labels: Marcelino, Escolá,
Lucia and Fuego. Jewellery by Pat
Whyte, Oky Coky

BARNARDO FURRIERS
108 Grafton St, Dublin 2, tel: 01
677 7867
Collection Designed by E. Barnardo

BIBAS BOUTIQUE
Main St, Malahide, Co. Dublin, tel:
01 845 1529, (10-18) 🧥 🧥
Labels: D'orsay, Gerry Weber,
Joseph Ribkoff, Linea Raffaelli and
Luis Civit

BLUE
51 Main St, Blackrock, Co. Dublin,
tel: 01 210 9939 (8-18) 👓 👞
⃝
Labels: 616 High, Marithé +
François Girbaud. Jewellery by
Reminiscence. Shoes by Marithé +
François Girbaud

BOLERO

2 Railway Road, Dalkey, Co.
Dublin, tel: 01 285 0104; (8-24)

Labels: Elsa Serrano, Merlina Ada,
Rapsodia and Toros Design

BOW

Powerscourt Townhouse Dublin 2,
tel: 01 7071763, Facebook, www.
bowpowerscourt.com (8-16)
Labels: Wendy's Wardrobe, Mo
Muse, Eilis Boyle, Lou Lou Belle,
Emma Manley

BOW AND PEARL

13 Main St, Ranelagh , Dublin 6 ,
tel: 01 496 7408,www.bowand-
pearl.com (8-16)
Labels: American Vintage, People
Tree, Darling, Nobody Denim

CHANTELLE FASHIONS

9a The Crescent, Monkstown, Co.
Dublin, tel: 01 280 3163, (8-18)

THE GABLES

Drumree, Dunshaughlin, Co.
Meath, tel: 8359943,
Labels: Basler, Escada Sport, Lau-
rél, Luisa Cerano and St John

CHICA

Unit 3-4, Westbury Mall, Dublin
2, tel: 01 633 4441; (6-14)
www.chicaboutiqueonline.com,
Facebook, twitter
Labels: Chica Boutique, Ella Luna,
Meghan, Lucas Jack, Dimtriatis,
Totem

COCO BOUTIQUE

40 Clarendon St, Dublin 2, tel:
01 8994300, www.cocoboutique.
ie, Facebook, (6-16)
Labels: Rubber Ducky, Hybrid,
La Evening Wear, Unze Couture,
Ruth Erotokritou.

COVET

Top Floor Powerscourt Cen-
tre, 59 South William St, Dublin
2, tel: 01 679 9313, www.covet.ie
(8-18)
Labels: Stella Mc Cartney, John
Galliano, Alexander McQueen,
Valentino, Christian Louboutin,
Oscar De La Renta, Prada

INDIGO AND CLOTH

www.indigoandcloth.com, Facebook
twitter (8-16)
Labels: V Ave Shoes Repair,
Oliver Spencer, Stylein, Dagmar,
Our Legacy

PAULA ROWAN

31 Westbury Mall, (off Grafton
St), Dublin 2, tel: 01 674 6662

Lables: Gloves - Paula Rowan,
bags, briefcases, luggage, belts and
accessories by Claudio Ferrici.

CAROUSEL

20 Exchequer St, Dublin 2, tel:
01 6778713, www.carouselvintage.
com, Facebook, twitter (8-16)
(v, Labels: vintage and vintage-
inspired clothing store.

CLOTHES PEG

Sutton Cross, Dublin 13, tel: 01
832 1130, Facebook (8-16)

Labels: Bleu Blanc Rouge, InWear,
Strenesse, Paul Smith, shoes and
bags by Sergio Rossi

COCOBELLE

Lord Mayor's Walk, Unit 25, Royal
Hibernian Way, Dawson St, Dublin
2, tel: 01 707 1818; www.cocobelle.
ie, Facebook (4-8)
Labels: Shoes by DKNY,
Givenchy, Michael Kors, Pretty
Ballerinas and Salvador Sapena

COMPAGNIE L

Merrion Centre, Dublin 4, tel: 01
260 1580, www.Compagniel.com

(8-16)
Labels: Timo, Stills, Finn Wright
Mason, Lucidez, Cara Lotti,

COSTUME

10-11 Castle Market, Dublin 2,
tel: 01 679 4188 (6-18)
Labels: Collette Dinnigan, Barbara
Bui, Isabel Marant, RM by Roland
Mouret, Temperley London, Anne
Valerie Hash, Dina Bar-El, Proenza
Schouler, Tadashi.

CYAN

Swan Centre, Rathmines, Dublin 6,
tel: 01 496 8681, Facebook (8-14)
Labels: Fornarina, Great Plains,
Roxy, Tara Jarmon, Custo, Isabel
De Pedro

DESIGN CENTRE

Powerscourt Centre, South William St, Dublin 2, tel: 01 679 5718,
01 679 586 (6-16)
Labels: Jasmine Di Milo, John
Rocha, La Petite Salope, Preen,
Black Halo, Accessories by Erickson Beamon

DIFFUSION

47 Clontarf Road, Dublin 3, tel: 01
833 1592 (8-16)
Labels: D&G, High, John Rocha,
Marithé + François Girbaud, Schumacher, Alice San Diego

DIVINE

Strand St, Malahide, tel: 01 845
3525; www.divine.ie (8-16)
Labels: See by Chloé, Kate & Ava,
Totem, Valentino Red, Voom, Issue
New York, Karen Brost, La Label,
Momalicious

DOLLS
14a Emorville Avenue, Dublin 8, tel: 01 4736256; www.dolls.ie (8-14)
Labels: Sessun, Dolls Label, Samatha Sung, YMC, Peter Jensen

DRESS CIRCLE
136 Terenure Road North, Terenure, Dublin 6, tel: 01 490 4115, (10-16)
Labels: Annette Görtz, Via Appia, Steilmann, Save The Queen

EMME
36 Dunville Avenue, Ranelagh, Dublin 6, tel: 01 497 1771, Facebook (3-8)
Labels: Shoes by Alberto Zago, Jaime Mascaró, Marco Moreo, Pretty Ballerinas

FITZPATRICKS SHOES
76 Grafton St, Dublin 2, tel: 01 677 2333; Unit 3, Level 1 Dundrum Town Centre, Dublin 14, tel: 01 298 3270; Units 5 & 6 Custom House Quay, IFSC, Dublin 1, tel:01 859 0370, www.fitzpatricksshoes.com (3-8)
Labels: Ladies' shoes by Dior, DKNY, Marc Jacobs, Ugg, Ralph Lauren, Sergio Rossi, Valentino

FRIZZANTE
99a Rathgar Road, Rathgar, Dublin 6, tel: 01 490 3768, (8-18)
Labels: Eroke, Lauren Vidal, Sotto Marino, James Lakeland, Divas

HAVANA
2 Anglesea House, Donnybrook, Dublin 4, tel:01 260 2707, www.havanaboutique.ie, Facebook, (8-14)
Labels: Ann Demeulemeester, Comme des Garçons, John Rocha, Rick Owens, Yohji Yamamoto, jewellery by Erickson Beamon

INGENUE
Unit 25, Westbury Mall, Dublin 2, tel: 01 6719836 Facebook (8-18)
Labels: Ingénue Label

KELLI
45 Ranelagh Village, Ranelagh, Dublin 6, tel: 01 497 0077, (8-14)
Labels: Amaya Arzuaga, Notruna, Essentiel, Marilyn Moore, Bombshell

KHAN
15 Rock Hill, Main St, Blackrock, Co. Dublin, tel:01 278 1646, Facebook (8-18)
Labels: Paul Smith Black Label, Schumacher, Fabiana Filippi, René Lezard, Marithé +François Girbaud

LARA
1 Dame Lane, Dublin 2, tel:01 670 7951; 15 Terenure Place, Terenure, Dublin 6W, tel: 01 499 1622; www.laras.ie, Facebook (8-16)
Labels: Burberry, Guess, J Brand, Just Cavalli, Tag, True Religion

LISA PERKINS
Unit 44, Blackrock Centre, Co. Dublin, tel: 01 288 4812, (10-20)
Labels: Bianca, Gelco, Gerry Weber, Not Your Daughter's Jeans, Twist, Lady Augusta

LOULERIE
14b Chatham St, Dublin 2, tel: 01 672 4024; www.loulerie.ie
Labels: Jewellery by Alexis Bittar, Judith Haas, Me & Ro, Nashelle, Town & Country, Archive, Patricia Nicolás

MAD HATTER
20 Lower Stephen St, Dublin 2, tel: 01 405 4936; www.madhatter.com
Labels: Hats by Atelier Autruch, Céline Robert, Godiva and Marzi. Jewellery by Pat Whyte, Kristina M and Murmure

MARIAN GALE
8 The Mall, Donnybrook, Dublin 4, tel: 01 269 7460, www.mariangale.ie, Facebook (10-20)
Labels: Giorgio Grati, Helen Marina, Martinelli, Precious Jeans and Valentina Barberini

MAVEN BOUTIQUE
64 Aungier St, Dublin 2, tel: 014789226, Facebook, (8-14)
Labels: Sian Jacobs, Unicorn, Talula De La Lune, Urbahia, Samantha Pleet, Garde, Yoon, Pepper and Pistol, Silvia Hilman, Bespoke jewellery by Ms Beatty.

MISS E
57 Glasthule Road, Sandycove, Co. Dublin, tel: 01 280 9849, www.misse.ie (8-16)
Labels: Isabel de Pedro, Mr Cat, Marc O'Polo, Sarah Pacini, Save The Queen, Turnover

NELO MATERNITY
39 Clarendon St, Dublin 2, tel: 01 679 1336; www.nelomaternity.com
Labels: Maternity by Citizens Of Humanity, Cocoon, Fragile, Juicy Couture, Veronique Delachaux, Belly Button, Queen Mom

NEOLA
Malahide Main St, Malahide, Co. Dublin, tel: 01 845 6033; Dundrum Shopping Centre, tel: 01 6853870, Dundalk: River Lane, Dundalk, Co. Louth, tel: 042 9335828, www.neola.ie (8-16)
Labels: 7 For All Mankind, French Connection, Ugg, Fornarina, Miss Sixty. Accessories by Guess

NOA NOA
34 South Ann St, Dublin 2, tel: 01672 9480, www.noanoaireland.com facebook (10-16) ◯ 👓
Labels: the full collection from Noa Noa

+PACE 3
Brighton Road, Foxrock, Dublin 18, tel: 01 289 7658; www.paceboutiques.com (8-18) ▲ 👕 ◯ 🐕
Labels: Ronen Chen, Marooned, Whisker, Heather Finn, European Couture

ROCCO OF CLONTARF
196 Clontarf Road, Dublin 3, tel: 01 853 0299, Facebook (8-18) ▲ ◯ 👟
Labels: Fenn Wright Manson, Isabel de Pedro, Mr Cat, James Lakeland, Save The Queen

SANDZ
23 Dunville Avenue, Ranelagh, Dublin 6, tel: 01 412 6514; (8-20) 👓 ◯
Labels: Eva Kayan, Sunlight, Peruzzi ,Frank Lyman

SANS SOUCI
The Green, Malahide, Co. Dublin, tel: 01 845 7630, (8-18) ▲
Labels: Aideen Bodkin, Talbot Rhunoff, by Timo, Sharo, Azcona

SEAGREEN
6a The Crescent, Monkstown, Co. Dublin, tel: 01 202 0130; www.seagreen.ie (10-16) ◯ 👟 ▲ 👓
Labels: Paul & Joe, Iro, Goat, K Brant, Victoria Beckham, Denim, Vince

SELECT BOUTIQUE
3 Farmhill Road, Goatstown, Dublin 14, tel:01 298 2073, Facebook (10-18) ▲ ▲ ◯
Labels: Just B, Via Appia, Evelin Brandt, Sandwich, James Lakeland

SERENA BOUTIQUE

Unit 3 Sandymount Road, Dublin 4, tel:01 667 6108; Frascati Centre, Blackrock, Co. Dublin, tel: 01 278 1050, Bloomfield Shopping Centre, tel: 01 284 3818 (8-20) 👕 ▲ 👓 ◯
Labels: Airfield, Elisa Cavaletti, Lauren Bidal, Mais il est où le Soleil?, Marc Cain Sport

SHAMON
Unit 2, Ashleigh Centre, Main St, Castleknock, Dublin 15, tel: 01 822 0588, Facebook (8-18) 👟 ◯
Labels: Bleu Blanc Rouge, James Lakeland, Indies, Isabel de Pedro. Shoes by Moda in Pelle. Jewellery by Dyrberg/Kern,

SOUL DESIGNS
2 Glasthule Road, Sandycove, Co. Dublin, tel: 01 280 8895; (8-16) 👜 👟 ◯
Labels: Chiemihara, Shoes by Oudley, To Be, Marco Moreo, Paco.

STEPZ SHOE BOUTIQUE
Main St, Malahide, Co. Dublin, tel: 01 845 6883; www.stepz.ie 👟 ◯ (4-8)
Labels: Shoes by Alberto Zago, Castaner, Pons Quintana, Robert Clergerie, Rucoline, Barbara Schwarzer, Gabi Lauton. Bags by Bicoli. Shoes by Pedro García and Roberto Del Carlo

SUSAN HUNTER LINGERIE
13 Westbury Mall, Grafton St, Dublin 2, tel: 01 679 1271; www.susanhunter.ie 👙
Labels: Lingerie by Aubade, Caoimhe O'Dwyer, Hanro, La Perla, Lejaby, And God Created Woman, Elixir, Rapture

THE TURRET
2-3 Castle Market, Dublin 2, tel: 01 671 4936, www.theturretboutique.com (8-20) ◯ 👟 ▲
Labels: John Charles, Linea Raffaelli, Maria Coca, Ian Stuart, Jaego

THOMAS PATRICK
77 Grafton St, Dublin 2, tel: 01 671 3866 (3-8) 👟 ◯
Labels: Shoes and Bags by Bruno Magli, Gabor, KMB, Peter Kaiser, Stuart Weitzman, Shoes by Rucoline

NEVER BLUE
Unit 7, Sutton Centre, Sutton Cross, Dublin 13, tel: 01 832 2234; (8-20) ▲ 👕 ◯
Labels: Never Blue, Lila B, Roze Enco, K Copper, Sunlight,

TRÈS CHIC
2a Main St, Malahide, Co. Dublin, tel: 01 845 0139, Facebook (8-16) 👓 ◯ 👟
Labels: by Malene Birger, Day, Birger et Mikkelsen, Indies, Lauren Vidal, Hoss Intropia

TYRRELL & BRENNAN
13 Lower Pembroke St, Dublin 2, 01 678 8332; www.tyrrellbrennan.com (8-18) ▲ ▲
The Tyrrell & Brennan Label, offering day tailoring, occasion, evening and bridal wear

VENEZUELA
86 Strand St, Skerries, Co. Dublin, tel: 01 849 0982, Facebook (8-16) 👓 ▲ ◯ 👟
Labels: Hoss Intropia, Isabel de Pedro, Mr Cat, James Lakeland, Sarah Pacini, Mc, Planet,

THE WHITE DOOR
14 Exchequer St Dublin.2, tel: 01 604 0034; Dunleer, Co. Louth, tel: 041 686 3640, www.thewhitedoor.ie, (Facebook, twitter) (8-16)
Labels, Hello!Skinny Jeans, DL1961, Premium Denim, Heidi Higgins, Carol Shaw Jewellery, Zorina Cosmetics

LEINSTER

ARIA BOUTIQUE
7 Poplar Square, Naas, Co. Kildare, tel: 045 871333; www.ariaboutique.ie, Facebook, twitter (8-16)
Labels: by Malene Birger, Charli, Tara Jarmon, Elisabelle Perde, Vivienne Westwood

ASHANTI GOLD
Esmonde St, Gorey, Co. Wexford, tel: 053 942 0342, Meridian Point, Greystones, Co. Wicklow, tel: 01 287 1789, Facebook (10-22)
Labels: Basler, Gant, Oky Coky, Sandwich, Creenstone

BARONESSA
Leinster St, Athy, Co. Kildare, tel: 059 863 8720, www.baronessa.ie, Facebook, twitter (8-16)
Labels: Day Birger et Mikkelsen, Gabor, Marco Moreo, Marc O'Polo, Sandwich, French Connection, Ikks, Oui Set

BELLA
67 Narrow West St, Drogheda, Co. Louth, tel: 041 983 4047, Facebook (8-16)
Labels: by Malene Birger, Stills, B&Sh, Javier Simora, Olivia

BLOSSOM TIME
Lyster House, Portlaoise, Co. Laois, tel: 057 8622882 (10-20)
Labels: Alaven, Via Veneto, Pratesi Robe, Frank Lyman, Dolce Vita, Olsen, Lebek

BRASS RAIL
86-87 Clanbrassil St, Dundalk, Co. Louth, tel: 042 933 0303 (8-16)
Labels: Set, One Step, Part Two, Pennyblack, InWear

BURGESS OF ATHLONE
1-7 Church St, Athlone, Co. Westmeath, tel: 090 647 2005; www.burgessofathlone.ie, Facebook, (8-22)
Labels: Eastex, Gerry Weber, Jacques Vert, Libra, Betty Barclay

CAZA CHOO SHOE BOUTIQUE
72 High St, Kilkenny, tel: 056 779 0592, Facebook, (3-8)
Labels: Modain Pelle, Luciano Barachini, Victora Deles, Omosa .

CHANTELLE
The Gables, Dunshaughlin, Co. Meath, tel: 01 825 9943 (10-20)
Labels: Basler, Escada Sport, Laurel, Luisa Cerano, St John

CHIC UNIQUE
Corballis Shopping Centre, Ratoath, Co.. Meath, tel: 01 825 7670. www.chicunique.ie (8-18)
Labels: InWear, Summum, Luke Lovely, Anoushka G, Damo, Classic Cut Clothing,

CLARA ELLEN
49 Dublin St, Longford, tel: 04333 48361; 33 Church St, Athlone, Co. Westmeath, tel: 090 647 4992; 1 Castle St, Mullingar, Co. Westmeath, tel: 044 934

4255, Facebook (6-18)
Labels: Fee G, Fenn Wright Manson, Rinascimento, Siste, La Rochelle

CLASSIC FX
Meridian Point Shopping Centre, Wicklow, Co. Wicklow, tel: 01 287 1801 (3-8)
Labels: Fitflop, Emu, Solo Soprani, Bulaggi, David Jones

COCO PINK
7 William St, Kilkenny, tel: 056 770 3705 (3-8)
Labels: Barbara Bui, Lara Bohinic, Gina, Magrit & Rodo, Lulu Guinness, Pictonna

CONTRA CLOTHING
99 Main St, Gorey, Co. Wexford, tel: 053 942 0189, www.contraclothing.com, Facebook, (8-16)
Labels: Dept, Mexx, Naf Naf, Part Two, Pepe, Desigual

CRAVE BOUTIQUE
1 Castle Buildings, Friary Road, Naas, Co. Kildare, tel: 045 883424, www.craveshoeboutique.ie, Facebook, (3-8)
Labels: DKNY, Gerard Darel, Selected Femme, Fenn Wright Manson, Oky Coky

DIVINE
Unit 3 Manor Mills Shopping Centre, Maynooth, Co. Kildare, tel: 01 629 2550; www.divine.ie Facebook (8-16)
Labels: Kate & Ava, See by Chloé, Totem, Valentino Red, Voom, New York, Karen Brost, La Label and Momalicious

EDEL'S BOUTIQUE

Unit 2 Kelton House, Lyster Square, Portlaoise, Co. Laois, tel: 057 866 0059; www.edelsboutique.com, Facebook (10-16)

LABELS: 7 FOR ALL MANKIND, FENN WRIGHT MANSON

Marc O'Polo, Ted Baker and Tommy Hilfiger, Citizens of Humanity, Esprit, Page Premium, Set, Soaked In Luxury

EDEN

90 Clanbrassil St, Dundalk, Co. Louth, tel: 042 938 6739; www.edenireland.com, Facebook, (8-16)

Labels: Orla Kiely, Sonia by Sonia Rykiel, Vanessa Bruno, Athe, Antik Batik

ELAINE CURTIS

Unit 6, Exchequer House, Poatato Market House, 122 Tullow St, Carlow, tel: 059 914 1790; www.elainecurtis.ee, Facebook (8-16)

Labels: Hoss Intropia, Sonia by Sonia Rykiel, Tim Ryan, Diane Von Furstenberg, Philosophy Di Alberta Ferretti

EMPORIUM KALU

16 South Main St, Naas, Co. Kildare, tel: 045 896222, Facebook (8-14)

Labels: Jenny Packham, Josep Font, Luella, Missoni, Vivienne Westwood Red Label.

ERRE ESSE

Mount Wolseley Hotel, Tullow, Co. Carlow, tel: 059 918 0117; Church St, Portlaoise, Co. Laois, tel: 057 868 2375; (8-16)

Labels: Aideen Bodkin, by Malene Birger, Custo, Matilde Cano,

Nougat, Manoush, Ugo Zaldi

ESCAPE

Church Road, Greystones, Co. Wicklow, tel: 01 287 1524, www.escapeboutique.com, Facebook, twitter (8-22)

Labels: Just B, Michael H, Noa Noa, Noli, Nu Women, Gustav

FABIANI

12 Grafton Court, Longford, tel: 04333 46049, Facebook, (3-8)

Labels: Shoes by Ash, KMB, Marco Moreo, Gianni Di Firenze, Le Babe .

FABUCCI

10 The Moat Mall, Naas, Co. Kildare, tel: 045 874721, www.fabucci.ie, Facebook, (3-8)

Labels: Shoes by Gabor, Marco Moreo, Pedro Anton, Marian, Gino Vaello

FISHERS

The Old Schoolhouse, Newtownmountkennedy, Co. Wicklow, tel: 01 281 9404; www.fishers.ie, (10-18)

Labels: Olsen, Styleman, Via Appia, Jack Murphy, Tulcan

FRENCH CONNECTION

Strand Road, Rosslare, Co. Wexford, tel: 053 913 2189 (10-18)

Labels: High, Marithé + François Girbaud, Zerres, Pataugas

GENEVIÈVE COX

4 Dublin St, Longford, tel: 043 33 40777, www.genivievecox.com (3-7)

Labels: David Jones, Solo Soprani, Passigatti, Whitley, About Face.

GIORGIO'S SHOE BOUTIQUE

1 Hillside Road, Greystones, Co. Wicklow, tel: 01 201 7252, Facebook, (3-7)

Labels: Le Babe, Rirker, Joni, KMB, Brouno Permi.

GLAMOUR

26 Main St, Enniscorthy, Co. Wexford, tel: 053 923 8144, Facebook, (8-20)

Labels: Jackpot, Tommy Hilfiger, Gant, Qui, Mills

HEAVEN BOUTIQUE

Marshes Shopping Centre, Dundalk, Co. Louth, tel: 042 935 1336, Facebook, (8-18)

Labels: Graffic, Stella, Layers, Toxic, Attentive

HEAVENLY

Main St, Clane, Co. Kildare, tel: 045 861719, Facebook (3-8)

Labels: Shoes by Lisa Kay, Smith Canova , Rock Reptile, Sacha London.Fiorelli

HEELS BOUTIQUE

Main St, Ashford, Co. Wicklow, tel: 0404 42701; www.heels.ie (3-8)

Labels: Fitflops, Marco Moreo, Marco Tozzi, Rieker and Tommy Hilfiger, Ash, Dream Masks, Envirosack, Pat Whyte and Tipsy Feet

KADEE BOUTIQUE

Pearse St, Athlone, Co. Westmeath, tel: 090 649 8355; www.kadee.ie (8-18)

Labels: Cricot Chic, Linea Raffaelli, Novia d'Art, Ritva Westenius. Fenn Wright Mason Lili Costa, Oky Coky, Chic, Jovani, Schumacher, Shine

JENNY TURNER
The Village Centre, Enniskerry, Co. Wicklow, tel: 01 286 1899, www.jennyturner.ie, (8-18)
Labels: Crea Concept, Gustav, Sandwich, Transit, Ronen Chen

JENNY'S BOUTIQUE,
Main St, Ashbourne, Co. Meath, tel:01 835 0782; Main St, Dunshaughlin, Co. Meath, tel: 01 824 0058, www.jennys.ie, Facebook, twitter (8-20)
Labels: Marc Cain, Isabel de Pedro, Marella, Ian Stuart, John Charles

JO DUGGAN
3 William St, Kilkenny, tel: 056 772 2217, Facebook, (10-18)
Labels: Gerard Darel, Marella,Tara Jarmon, Schumacher, Moloko

JUJU
Unit 3, La Touche Place, Greystones, Co. Wicklow, tel: 01 201 6723, www.juju.ie, Facebook (8-16)
Labels: Joseph, Schumacher, Sphere One, Velvet, Sportmaxx,

KABELO BOUTIQUE
Emmet Square, Birr, Co. Offaly, tel: 057 912 3812, Facebook, (8-18)
Labels: Almost Famous, James Lakeland, Pennyblack, Salsa Jeans

KASURA
12 High St, Ashbourne, Co. Meath, tel: 01 835 7913, www.kasura.ie, Facebook, (8-22)
Labels: Fever, Darling, Stop Straing, Part Two, Nu Staff,

KHAN
27 Dominic St, Mullingar, Co. Westmeath, 044 939 6908, Facebook, www.khan.ie (8-16)
Labels: J Brand Jeans, Marithé + François Girbaud, 7 Jeans, Velvet .

LAURA GRAY BOUTIQUE
Shopping Centre, Church Road, Tullamore, Co. Offaly, 057 934 1886, Facebook, (10-18)
Labels:, Bandolera, Marc Aurel, Frank Lyman, Joseph Ribkoff, Olsen

LURE
51 Dublin St, Longford, 043 33 48484, (8-18)
Labels, Kaliorea, My Soul, Expression, Hybrid, Ya Ya

LYNCH'S LADIES BOUTIQUE
Main St, Banagher, Co. Offaly, 057 915 1380; www.lynchfashions.com, Facebook, (8-18)
Labels: Carla Ruiz, Ian Stuart, John Charles, Mareia, Maria Coca, Condici.

MAKABA
53 The Avenue, Whitewater Shopping Centre, Newbridge, Co. Kildare, 045 432919; www.makaba.ie (10-18)
Labels: 7 For All Mankind, Leona Edmiston, Munthe Plus Simonsen, Unconditional, Willow

MILAN & CO.
11 Florence Road, Bray, Co. Wicklow, 01 286 6733; www.milan-co.com (8-16)
Labels: by Malene Birger, Hoss Intropia, James Lakeland, O.Titude and Pocket Venus, Blank and Qi

NATTERJACKTOAD
Castle St. Mullingar, Co. Westmeath, tel: 044 93 45676 (Facebook) (8-16)
Labels: Firetrap, Emily & Fin, Supremebeing, Mink Pink, Superdry

MIMI BOUTIQUE
4 Crian St, Kilkenny, tel: 056 7751001, Facebook, (8-16)
Labels: Pennyblack, by Meelab Merber, Turnover, Sandwich, Summum

MIRO SHOES
2 Adelphi Mall, The Longwalk, Dundalk, Co. Louth, tel: 042 933 3620; www.miroshoes.net, Facebook, (3-8)
Labels: Shoes by DKNY, Marco Moreo, Marian, Sachelle, Gibellieri,

NEOLA RIVER LANE
Dundalk, Co. Louth, tel: 042 933 5828; www.neola.ie, Facebook (8-16)
Labels: Diesel, French Connection, Odd Molly and Ted Baker, Guess

NICOLA ROSS
1a North Main St, Naas, Co. Kildare, tel: 045 875181, www.nicolaross.ie, Facebook, (8-22)
Labels: Linea Raffaelli, Luis Civit, Fee G, inspirato, Kate and Pippa.

OLIVIA DANIELLE
19 Church St, Athlone, Co. Westmeath, tel: 090 647 2707, www.oliviadanielle.com, Facebook (8-18)
Labels: Moschino, Marcelino, Weill, Escada, Just Cavalli

OONA CONROY
120 Tullow St, Carlow, tel: 059 913 9777, www.oonaconroy.com, Facebook, twitter (3-8)
Labels: KMB, Guess, Decode, Lisa Kay, Le Babe

OTTIVA
2 Weafer St, Enniscorthy, Co. Wexford, tel: 053 923 8840, (8-16) Labels: Indies, Legatte, Nue, LaFee, Pennyblack,

PALUA BOUTIQUE
Main St, Leixlip, Co. Kildare, tel:
01 624 2711; www.paluaboutique.
ie, Facebook, (8-18) 🔺👕
Labels: InWear, Jackpot, Alse
Jacobsen, No Man's Land,
Sandwich

PASMA SHOES
2 Irish St, Ardee, Co. Louth, tel:
041 685 8511; www.pasmashoes.
com, Facebook, (3-8) ⚪👞
Labels: Shoes by Marco Moreo,
Sachelle Couture, Marian, Pedro
Anton, Lulu Guinness

ROSS MORGAN
Yew Tree Square, Prosperous
Road, Co. Kildare, 045 902162;
www.rossmorgan.ie (16-30) 👗👞
⚪
Labels: Anna Scholtz, Apart, Doris
Streich, Elena Grunert, Yoek,
Ember Blossom

RUBY ROUGE
The Doll's House Esmonde St,
Gorey, Co.Wexford, tel: 053 94
84722, www.rubyrouge.ie, Face-
book, (8-16) 🔺⚪
Labels: Rubber Ducky, Marcelino,
Hoss Intropia, by Malene Birger,
Doll by Ruby Rouge

SCRUPLES
8 South Main St, Naas, Co. Kildare, tel: 045 901734, Facebook
(8-18) 🔺👕⚪
Labels: James Lakeland, Tomo, No
Man's Land, Sandwich, All Most
Famous

SERENDIPITY BOUTIQUE
34 Kieran St, Kilkenny, tel:056
775 6839, www.serendipitybou-
tique.ie, Facebook (8-20) 🔺👗
Labels: Fee G, Fran & Jane, Hello
Skinny Jeans, Rubber Ducky, Rise
Boutique

SHADORE
Meridian Point, Greystones, Co.
Wicklow, tel: 01 287 5999, www.
shadore.com, Facebook, (8-16)
👕🕶️👗
Labels: Legatte, Mais il est où le
Soleil? Obi, Rosemarie R, Vassalli

THE DESIGNER EXCHANGE
SWAP SHOP
Unit 1 Primrose Forge, Hazelhatch
Road, Celbridge, Co. Kildare, tel:
01 654 4358;
www.thedesignerexchange.net,
Facebook, (8-18) 🦌
Labels: Armani, Chanel, Jimmy
Choo, Manolo Blahnik, Miu Miu

TIGER LILY BOUTIQUE
Oliver Plunkett St, Oldcastle, Co.
Meath, tel: 049 855 0818, Face-
book, , (8-18) 🔺👕⚪
Labels: Kate Copper, Dec, Avalon,
Pruzzi, Flare Line

TOIL AND GLITTER
The Main Street, Greystones, Co.
Wicklow, tel: 01 201 7426; Rail
Road, Dalkey, Co. Dublin, tel: 01
2848004, www.toilandglitter.com,
Facebook, (8-14) 👕🔺
Labels: one Step, Hunky Dory,
twist tango, Moloko and Odd Molly

UTOPIA BOUTIQUE LTD
Market Place, Main St, Dun-
shaughlin, Co. Meath, tel: 01 825
8844, www.utopiaboutique.ie,
Facebook, (8-16) 👕🔺
Labels: High, Hoss Intropia, Mary
Grant, Lauren Bidal, by Malene
Birger, White Stuff,

VANITY FAIR
Unit 3, The Courtyard Shopping
Centre, Newbridge, Co. Kildare,
tel: 045 431905, www.vanityfair.ie,
Facebook, (10-25) 👗🔺
Labels: Condici, Maria Coca, Luis
Civit, Max Mara, Aideen Bodkin

WARDROBE
Fitzwilliam Square, Wicklow, tel:
0404 68649, Facebook, www.
heels.ie (3-8) 👞⚪
Labels: Desigual, Jus d'Orange,
Salsa Jeans, Daisy May, Gabor
Shoes,

MUNSTER

AVA & ANNA'S
6 Tramway Terrace, Douglas Vil-
lage, Co. Cork, tel: 021 436 2231,
Facebook, (8-18) 🔺
Labels: Aftershock, Naf Naf, So
Couture, Nicole Miller and Nougat
London

BAMBOO
The Cottage, Ardfert Village,
Tralee, Co. Kerry, tel: 066 711
5915, Facebook, (10-18) 👜
Labels: Knit by D, Emily and Finn,
Aftershock, Ceci Tokyo, Avoca

BELLA SOLA
4 Bishop St, Newcastlewest, Co.
Limerick, tel: 069 78222, www.
bellasola.com, Facebook (6-16) 🔺
👕
Labels: Fehu, Isabel de Pedro, Ted
Baker, Nicole Miller, Pennyblack,

CALI WOMENSWEAR
Broderick St, Midleton, Co. Cork,
021 463 1999 (6-18) 👞👗
Labels: Moloko, One Step, Sarah
Pacini, Arianna, Daisy May

COCO
41 William St, Listowel, Co. Kerry,
tel: 068 23069, www.cocolistowel.
com, Facebook (10-18) 🔺👕
Labels: Fee G, Fenn Wright Manson, Marcelino, St One, The Barn .

COUNTY BOUTIQUE

57 O'Connell St Ennis, tel: 065 6821947, www.countyboutique. com, Facebook, , (8-16)
Labels:, Aideen Bodkin, Marc Cane, Olsen, Michael H Gold, White Stuff

CHIC BOUTIQUE

2 Church St Listowel, Co. Kerry, 068 21155, www.chicboutique.ie, (10-18)
Facebook Labels:, Bluetime Fashion, Linda Wilson, Wolford, Zeddra

EALÚ

15 Percival St, Kanturk, Co. Cork, tel: 029 20866, Facebook (8-16)
Labels: French Connection, Noa Noa, One Step, Almost Famous, James Lakeland

CROWNING GLORY

Percival St, Kanturk Co. Cork, (Facebook)
Labels: Anonymous, Stella, sophyline, Epilogue, Fever

EDEL'S BOUTIQUE

Friar St, Nenagh, Co. Tipperary, tel: 067 43186; www.edelsboutique.com, Facebook, twitter (8-16)
Labels:, 7 For All Mankind, Fenn Wright Manson, Marc O'Polo, Ted Baker, Esprit

EFFIGY

14 Russell St, Tralee, Co. Kerry, tel: 066 712 0938, Facebook, (8-18)
Labels: Almost Famous, French Connection, Olga Berg, Almatrichi, Naf Naf,

ELA MARIA

The Square House, Newcastlewest, Co. Limerick, tel:069 62855; 4 Salt House Lane, Ennis, Co. Clare, 065 684 2873; 9 Rock St, Tralee, Co. Kerry, 066 712 3230, www.elamaria.ie, Facebook, (8-24)
Labels: Airfield, Basler, 22 Maggio, Pinko, missoni

FLAX IN BLOOM

Cruises St, Limerick, tel: 061 318891 (8-16)
Labels: InWear, Jackpot, Part Two, Sandwich, Noa Noa, The Burn

FOOTSTEPS

Croke St, Thurles, Co. Tipperary, tel:0504 26747; www.footstepsshoes.ie, Facebook (3-8)
bags, shoes, accessories and umbrellas exclusive to Footsteps

GOOSEBERRY

54 Mccurtian Hill, Clonakilty, Co. Cork, tel: 023 8835812, Facebook. (8-16)
Labels: Hoss Intropia, S'nob, White Stuff, Timo, St-Martins

JOANNE'S FASHION HOUSE

Ballina, Killaloe, Co. Clare, tel:061 375735, (8-18)
Labels: Luis Civit, Marc O'Polo, Kate Copper, Forever Unique, Ann Balon

KATIE JANE'S

Castletroy Shopping Centre, Castletroy, Limerick, tel: 061 333739 (8-22)
Labels: Desigual, Fee G, Peruzzi, St One, Yoek, Libra, Steilmann

KATWALK BOUTIQUE

Collbawn, Broderick St, Midleton, Co. Cork, tel: 021 461 3036, Facebook, ,(8-18)
Labels: Lisa Cavaletti, Gardeur, Fred Sabatier, Nissa, Easy Comfort

KELLY'S

75-76 The Quay, Waterford, tel: 051 873557 (10-20)

Labels: Basler, Gerry Weber, Fenn Wright Manson, Joseph Ribkoff, Michael H

KERRYS BOUTIQUE

75 High St Killarny Co. Kerry, www.kerrysboutique.com, Facebook, twitter, (8-18)
Labels: Philip Treacy, Heidi Higgs, Caroline Kilkenny, Ruby Ray, Matilde Cano

KIMONO NORTH QUAY

Newcastlewest, Co. Limerick, tel: 069 78820;
Main St, Charleville, Co. Cork, tel: 063 21602; www.kimono.ie, Facebook, (8-18)
Labels: by Malene Birger, Hoss Intropia, Matildo, Tara Jarmon, Fuego, Oky Koky

KWILLA

23 Rose Inn St, Kilkenny, tel: 056-7806261, www.kwilla.eu
Labels: ABoxForMyTreasure, Arty Smarty, Fay's Studio, Hannah Davies, Tatty Devine

LA BOHÈME

Green St, Dingle, Co. Kerry, tel: 066 915 2444, Facebook, (6-18)
Labels: Fenn Wright Manson, Noa Noa, St-Martins, French Connection, Fee Gee.

LE CHÂTEAU

Liberty Square, Thurles, Co. Tipperary, tel: 0504 26535, (8-16)
Labels: Airfield, Bleu Blanc Rouge, Isabel de Pedro, Armati, Nougat .

LUCA

30 Prince's St, Cork, tel: 021 427 0440 (4-7)
Labels: Shoes by Coccinelle, L'autre Chose, K&S, Pedro García and Pura Lopez

MACBEES
25 New St, Killarney, Co. Kerry, tel: 064 33622; www.macbees.ie, (8-20)
Labels: Crea Concept, by Malene Birger, Aideen Bodkin, Sarah Pacini, Hoss Intropia, Tara Jarmon. Shoes by Chie Mihara

MARIE THERESE
4 The Mall, Thurles, Co. Tipperary, 0504 26791, Facebook, (8-18)
Labels: Mexx, Part Two, Sandwich, St One, White Stuff

MIRIAM HALLEY'S BOUTIQUE
Main Guard, 57 Gladstone St, Clonmel, Co. Tipperary, tel: 052 6127444, (8-16)
Labels: Aideen Bodkin, Desigual, InWear, N&C Kilkenny, Nicowa, Betty Boom, Eva Tralala, Laga, Sugarhill Boutique and White Stuff

MODA
Mallow 143 Bank Place Main St, Mallow, Co. Cork, tel: 022 42737, Facebook (8-16)
Labels: Avoca, Maison Stoch, cath kidston, Noa Noa, Sandwich

MON AMIE
Main St, Killarney, Co. Kerry, (Facebook) (8-18)
Labels: Diva, So Couture, Glamorous, Laundry Room, Mon Amie Vintage

MUSE
92 The Quay, Waterford, 051 854448 Facebook (8-18)
Labels: by Malene Birger, Ginger & Smart, Hoss Intropia, Sass & Bide

NAPHISA BOUTIQUE
1st Floor, 4 Cook St, Cork, 021 427 3787, Facebook,
Labels: New and nearly new clothing by Armani, Fendi, Gucci, Ischiko and Prada, Chloé, D&G, Joanne Hynes, Paul Smith and Rick Owens

NELO MATERNITY
53 Roches St, Limerick, tel: 061 207146; www.nelomaternity.com,
Labels: Maternity by Rights, Citizens Of Humanity, Cocoon, Fragile, Belly Button and Queen Mom

NOZOMI
71 O'Connell St, Ennis, Co. Clare, tel: 065 682 8655; www. nozomishose.com, Facebook, (3-8)
Labels: Shoes by Alberto Zago, Abbabe, Rebeca Sanver, Guglielmo Rotta, Magrit

O'DWYER FOOTWEAR
65 Main St, Midleton, Co. Cork, tel: 021 463 1572; 114 Oliver Plunkett St, Cork, tel: 021 427 3949; 84 North Main St, Youghal, Co. Cork, tel: 024 90006; The Bridge Shopping Centre, Dungarvan, Co. Waterford, tel: 058 24806 75 (3-8)
Labels: Shoes by Gabor, Marco Moreo and Tommy Hilfiger, Argenta, KMB,

ORCHID BOUTIQUE
Unit 1, Ballinakill Shopping Centre, Dunmore Road, Waterford, tel:051 859360, www.orchidboutique-waterford.com, Facebook, (8-18)
Labels: Almost Famous, Custo Barcelona, Charo Azcona, InWear, Oky Coky

PERFECT PAIRS
10 Church St, Listowel, Co. Kerry, tel: 068 23773, Facebbok (3-8)
Labels: Iris, Marco Moreo, Marian, Paradox, s. Oliver, Pedro Anton

PLATFORM BOUTIQUE
Bridge St, Newcastlewest, Co. Limerick, tel: 069 786147, www. platform.ie, (8-20)
Labels: 7 For All Mankind, Stills, Turn Over, Orla Kiely,

RED LANE
The Cross, Tramore Co. Waterford., www.redlane.ie, Facebook, (8-16)
French Connection, Great Plains, Fee G, St-Martins, Darling, Sticky Fingers

SATINA
Queen St, Tramore, Co. Waterford, tel: 051 386600, Facebook, (8-16)
Labels: Armani, Kenzo, Missoni and Moschino, Amanda Wakeley

SHEENA'S BOUTIQUE
24 Oliver Plunkett St, Cork, tel: 021 427 0574; 85 Main St, Midleton, Co. Cork, www.sheenas.ie, (8-22)
Labels: Joseph Ribkoff, Save The Queen, Cool Femme, Creenstone, Sonia Pena

SHOE FLAIR
56 Roche's St, Limerick, tel: 061 318686; Mitchell St, Nenagh, tel: 067 37536; Market St, Ennis, tel: 065 689 3741; Bridge St, Newcastlewest, Co. Limerick, tel: 069 77755 (4-8)
Labels: Adrian Vidal, KMB, Marco Moreo, Marian, Stephanie Moreno and Toni Pons

SINEAD'S BOUTIQUE
Salmon Weir, Annacotty, Co. Limerick, tel: 061 339696, www. sineadsboutique.com, (8-18)
Labels: Santino, John Bentley, John Charles, Frank Lyman, Sandwich

KITTYJANES
Castletroy Shopping Centre
Limerick, tel: 061 333739, www.
kittyjanes.com, Facebook (8-22)

Labels:, Peruzzi, Fee G, Daisy
May, Steilmann, Via Appia

TAELANE BOUTIQUE
Tae Lane, Listowel, Co. Kerry, tel:
068 53885, Facebook

Stockists of bags, jewellery,
separates, lingerie and vintage-style
accessories

THE DRESSING ROOM
4 Emmet Place, Cork, tel: 021 427
0117; www.dressingroomonline.
com, (8-18)
Labels: Cinoche, Portfolio, René
Derhy, Marcelino and Sonia
Fortuna

THE WARDROBE
Clonmel, 37 Gladstone St,
Clonmel, Co. Tipperary, tel: 052
612 6922, Facebook (8-16)

Labels: Avoca Anthology, by
Malene Birger, Jackpot, Noa Noa,
Nougat, Lulu, Red, Totem and
St-Martins

WILD PAIR
5-6 Russell St, Tralee, Co. Kerry,
tel: 066 718 5675, Facebook

BELFAST
(When ringing Northern Ireland from
the Republic of Ireland, replace the
prefix 028 With 048.)

RIO BRAZIL
Wellington Place and Bradbury
Place, Belfast, tel: 028 9024
5552, (8-16)
Labels: 7 For All Mankind, High,
Isabel de Pedro Mr Cat, James
Jeans

CRUISE
Victoria Square, Belfast, tel: 028
9032 0550; www.cruiseclothing.
co.uk Facebook, (8-16)

Labels: Diane Von Furstenberg,
Victoria Beckham, Jimmy Choo,
Balenciaga, Chloé

FRAN & JANE
Unit 2, Lesley Plaza, Lisburn Road,
Belfast, tel:028 9068 7716; www.
franandjane.ie, (8-18)

Labels: Axara, Fran & Jane, Holly
Morgan and Robin's Jeans

HONEY
627 Lisburn Road, Belfast, tel:
028 9066 7466; www.honeycol-
lection.co.uk, Facebook, twitter,
(8-3)
Labels: Chie Mihara, Pedro
García, Lejaby, Myla, Lulu Guinness, Lotus Villas

ROJO SHOES
613 Lisburn Road, Belfast, tel:028
9066 6998; www.Rojoshoes.
Co.Uk, (3-8)
Labels: Clothing by Nolita, KNS,
Prada, Michael Kors DKNY,
Stuart Weitzman, Ugg

STATEMENT AT MARGARET
GIBONEY
527 Lisburn Road, Belfast, tel:
028 9066 4507, (3-8)
Labels: Ambiente, Iblues, Louisa
Cerano, René Lezard, St Émile.

THE VELVET BOUTIQUE
661 Lisburn Road, Belfast, tel: 028
9066 5221, www.velvetclothing.
co.uk, Facebook, (8-16)
Labels: Anna Sui, J Brand,
Laundry, Industry, Schumacher,
Tori Bruy

THE WHITE BICYCLE
50 Bloomfield Avenue, Belfast, tel:
028 9045 7719; www.thewhitebi-
cycle.co.uk, Facebook, (8-18)

Labels: Sarah Pacini, Transit, Sandwich, Oliva Ruben, Part Two

UNA RODEN COUTURE
50 Upper Arthur St, Belfast, tel:
028 9024 8811,
Labels: Una Roden, French designers

ULSTER
(When ringing Northern Ireland from
the Republic of Ireland, replace the
prefix 028 With 048.)

BERLING
28 The Mall, Ground Floor
Unit, Newry, Co. Down, www.
berling.co.uk, Facebook, (8-18)

Labels: Aftershock, Almost Famous, Arianna, Ella Boo, Hunters
& Gatherers

BERNADETTE ELIZABETH
22-24 Bridge St, Newry, Co.
Down, tel: 028 3026 0479, www.
bernadetteelizabeth.com (10-18)

Labels: DKNY, Paul Costelloe,
Sand, Sphere One, Theory, Al-
berta Ferretti, Dina Bar-El, Sarah
Danielle

CLARE CLOTHING
19 Academy Court, Letterkenny,
Co. Donegal, tel:074 916 7555,
(10-18)
Labels: Crea Concept, Oska, St
One, Aideen Bodkin,.

EDGE EMPORIUM

7-9 Market Square, Dungannon, Co. Tyrone, tel: 028 8772 7773, www.edgeemporium.co.uk. Facebook, (8-16) 👞 👞
Labels: Custo Barcelona, Dolce & Gabbana, Versace, Circle of gentlemen, Alice by Temperley

SILK

Drumalane Mill, The Quays, Newry, Co. Down, tel: 028 3083 5555, Facebook, (8-16) 👜 ◯
Labels: 7 For All Mankind, J Brand, Barbour, REDValentino

PROMISE AT MCELHINNEYS

Main St, Ballybofey, Co. Donegal, tel: 074 913 1217; www.mcelhinneys.com, Facebook, (10-20)
👕 👕 👞 ◯
Labels: Guess, Miss Sixty, Ted Baker and Tommy Hilfiger

SARETTA

17 Charlemont St, Moy, Co. Tyrone, tel: 028 8778 9955; www.sarettamoy.com, Facebook, Labels: Part Two, Pause Café, Ella Boo, Kate Copper

THE LINGERIE ROOM

7 The Linen Green, Moygashel, Dungannon, Co. Tyrone, tel: 028 8772 3181. www.thelingerieroom.com, 👙
Labels: Lingerie by Chantelle, La Perla, Marie-Jo and Prima Donna. Nightwear by Louis Féraud, Hosiery by Wolford

VANILLA

33-35 Church St, Cavan, tel: 049 437 2641 (10-16) 👜 ◯
Labels: Escada Sport, Laurèl, Nougat, Louisa Cerano

WEBSITES

www.theoutnet.com
www.boohoo.com
www.asos.com
www.dresses.ie
www.littlewoodsireland.ie
www.simplybe.ie
www.net-a-porter.com
www.topshop.com
www.stylistpick.com
www.my-wardrobe.com
www.style.com
www.yoox.com
www.jaeger.co.uk
www.isabellaoliver.com
www.apc.fr
www.toast.co.uk
www.urbanoutfitters.co.uk
www.zara.com
www.bunnyhug.co.uk
www.liberty.co.uk
www.my-wardrobe.com
www.pollyanna.com
www.shopatanna.co.uk
www.start-london.com
www.whistles.co.uk
wwwadili.com
www.howies.co.uk
www.black.co.uk

JEWELLERY

www.mawi.co.uk
www.alexmonroe.co.uk
www.astleyclarke.co.uk
www.blaguette.com
www.cristobal.co.uk
www.kabiri.co.uk

LINGERIE AND NIGHTWEAR

www.figleaves.co.uk
www.boudiche.co.uk
www.bravissimo.com
www.pyjamaroom.com
www.volgalinen.co.uk

BEAUTY

www.aesop.net.au
www.bobbi-brown.co.uk
www.boots.com
www.clinique.co.uk
www.comfortandjoy.co.uk
www.cultbeauty.co.uk
www.eyeslipsface.co.uk
www.hqhair.com
www.johnlewis.co.uk
www.lookfantastic.com
www.lovelula.com
www.puresha.com
www.screenface.com
www.spacenk.com
www.spiezia.co.uk

PLUS SIZES

www.curvylady.ie/
www.curvissa.co.uk
www.plussize.ie
www.oxendales.ie
www.yoursclothing.ie
www.longtallsally.com
www.marisota.co.uk
www.rossmorgan.ie
www.dreamdiva.com.au
www.kiyonna.com
www.ullapopken.com
www.style369.com
www.curvety.com
www.swakdesigns.com
www.sydneyscloset.com
www.annascholz.com

www.cherished-woman.com
http://carmakoma.com/da/
www.coleenbow.com
www.damnyoualexis.com.au
www.elenamiro.it
www.hopeandharvest.com
www.leonaedmiston.com
www.marinarinaldi.com
www.mossdesign.co.nz
www.stefaniebezaire.com
www.ashleystewart.com
www.citychiconline.com
www.eloquii.com
www.eshakti.com
www.chicstar.com
www.lanebryant.com
www.navabi.co.uk
www.onestopplus.com
www.swakdesigns.com
www.womanwithin.com

SHOE SITES

kurtgeiger.co.uk
lastfootwear.com

LARGE AND SMALL SIZE SHOE SITES

www.solecity.ie
www.fifibelle.com
www.bigshoeboutique.co.uk
www.cinderellashoes.ie
www.atlastshoes.com.au
www.barefoottess.com
www.crispinsshoes.com
www.totallylargeshoes.co.uk
www.bigonshoes.com.au

VINTAGE

JENNY VANDER
Drury St, Dublin 2, tel: 01 677 0406

SAVVY STYLE
Roxboro Mews, Midleton, Co. Cork, tel: 087 7615455

ELSA & GOGO
Derrigra, Ballineen, Co. Cork, tel: 086 322 5284 www.elsaand-gogoboutique.ie, Facebook

LOVE VINTAGE
Market St, Clifden, Co. Galway, Facebook

9 CROW ST
Temple Bar, Dublin 2, www.9crows.blogspot.com, Facebook

QUACK+DIRK
Marino Mart, Fairview .Dublin, http://www.quackanddirk.com Facebook

GODDESS ROOM
Meridian Point, Church Rd, Grey-stones, Co.. Wicklow tel: 01 201 6591, www.thegoddessroom.net

MISS DAISY BLUE
Unit 7 Market Parade, 51/53 Patrick St, Cork, tel: 021479428, Facebook

MERCURY GOES RETRO-GRADE
19c Drawbridge St, Cork, Ireland, tel: 087 135 1980, Facebook

TURQUOISE FLAMINGO
4 Washington St, Cork, tel: 087 7553302 www.turquoiseflamingo.com, Facebook

ENCHANTED VINTAGE CLOTHING
Benbulben Centre, Rathcormac, Co. Sligo, tel: 071 914 6680, www.vintageclothing.ie

PERSONAL SHOPPING

ARNOTTS
tel: 01 8045842, or email person-alshopping@arnotts.ie

BROWN THOMAS
tel: 01 6171108, or personalshop-ping@brownthomas.ie

DEBENHAMS
tel: 01 8909 46779 or www.debenhams.ie

TOPSHOP
tel: 1800535570 or book-ings@topshop.com Blanchard-stown Shopping Centre, tel: 0851014444 or email: info@personal-stylist.ie
Liffey Valley Shopping Centre, tel: 086 339 6419 or email info@styleuphoria.com

HOUSE OF FRASER
tel: 01 2991400 or www.houseof-fraser.co.uk

HARVEY NICHOLS
contact 01 2910488 Dundrum Shopping Centre, contact 01 299 1700

ALTERATIONS

A ALTERATIONS
35 Park St, Dundalk, Co. Louth, 0429333380

A STITCH IN TIME
8 Clonard St, Balbriggan, Co. Dublin, 086 1925486

A STITCH IN TIME
Main St, Wicklow Town, Co. Wicklow, 087 3207468

ALTERATION & SEWING SERVICE
3 Merchants sq, Ennis, Co. Clare, 065 6840500

ALTERATION SHOP THE
26 Roches St, Limerick, Co. Limerick, 061 414176

ALTERATIONS CRUISE PARK DRIVE,
Dublin 15, Co. Dublin, 086 36 88 538

ALTERED CLOTHING
355 Ballyfermot Rd, Dublin 10, Co. Dublin, 01 6239664

ANN RYAN DRESSMAKER
Emmet Place, Nenagh, Co. Tipperary, 086 8198108

ANNE GREGORY DESIGN
The Cottage, Newtownmountkennedy, Co. Wicklow, 01 201 1748 / 086 840 2214

AVENUE ALTERATIONS
Unit 1 Greenacres Shopping ctr, Dundalk, Co. Louth (042)9352348

BARRY'S TAILORING SERVICE
85 North Main St, Cork, Co. Cork, 0214278048

BITSEY SEWING SERVICES
7 Springfield, Fermoy, Co. Cork, 086 4088127

BIZZY LIZZY ALTERATIONS
Quinn's Road, Shankill, Co. Dublin 01 2820501

BOGART TAILORS
17 Capel St, Dublin 1, Co. Dublin, (1890)942221

BRENNAN MARY ALTERATIONS
16 Donabate town ctr, Donabate, Co. Dublin, 01 8434996

BYRNE, DES TAILORING ALTERATIONS LTD
4/5 Grafton St, Dublin 2, Co. Dublin, 01 6773821

CATHERINES SEWING SERVICE
Main St, Celbridge, Co. Kildare, 016276322

CLASSIC TAILORS
33 Nth Main St, Naas, Co. Kildare, 045 876696

CLOTHES DOCTOR THE
16 Academy St, Cork, Co. Cork, 021 4272442

CLOTHING ALTERATIONS
151a Drimnagh Rd, Dublin 12, Co. Dublin, 014556550

CLOTHING ALTERATIONS
103A New Cabra rd, Dublin 7, Co. Dublin, (01)8389405

CLOTHING ALTERATIONS
274 Ballyfermot rd, Dublin 10, Co. Dublin, 01 6230476

CRAFT CAFE @ FABRIC GALLERY
Church Terrace, Bray, Co. Wicklow, 01 2860979

CURTAIN MAKING & ALTERATIONS CENTRE
Bray, Co. Wicklow, 01-2022856

CUTTING IMAGE @ TALLON MENSWEAR
206 Harold's Cross Rd, Dublin 6, 01 4969503

DENISE'S XPRESS ALTERNATIONS
1a Fitzwilliam Row, Adjacent to Delahunts, Wicklow Town, 086 3171051

DILLON ANGELA
Main St, Charleville, Co. Cork, 063 89085

DONAGHMEDE ALTERATIONS
Unit 41 Donaghmede S.C., Dublin 13, 018484764

DOVE DRY CLEANING
Athgarvan Road, Newbridge, Co. Kildare, 045 444 010

DRESS MAKING & TAILORING AT STUDIO 54
54 Temple Rd, Blackrock, Co. Dublin 01 2789757

DRESSING ROOM THE
41-42 upr Gladstone st, Clonmel, Co. Tipperary, 05229552

DUNLAOGHAIRE ALTERATION TAILORS
64A Convent rd, Dun Laoghaire, Co. Dublin, 01 2802962

ELENA DORU COUTURE DESIGN STUDIO
Unit 19, The Groody Retail Centre, Castletroy, Co. Limerick, 087 786 2275

ELITE ALTERATIONS
Main St, Greystones, Co. Wicklow, 085 168 0341

EXCHANGE AND ALTER
Main St, Rathangan, Co. Kildare, 087 329 3530

EXPRESS ALTERATION TAILORS
53 Middle Abbey st, Dublin 1, 018730449

EXPRESS ALTERATIONS
56 Sth Main st, Naas, Co. Kildare, 045 875490

EXPRESS ALTERATIONS
1st Floor, 19 Rose Inn st, Kilkenny, 0567777415

FAST ALTERATIONS
15 Trimgate st, Navan, Co. Meath, 0469059979

FIRST CLASS DLA
59A Fairview Strand Fairview, Dublin 3, 01 8367151

GLENDALE
107 Barrack St, Cork, 0214316158

GRAFTON ALTERATIONS
7 South Anne St., Dublin 2, (01)6717813

GREGORY ANNE DESIGN
The Cottage, Newtown-mountkennedy, Co. Wicklow, 01 2011748

HERBIE ALTERATIONS
Unit 3 Village Gate Arcade, Bray, Co. Wicklow, 012723122

HERBIES ALTERATIONS
Arcade, Bray, Co. Wicklow, 01 2723122

HIS & HERS
Bray, Co. Wicklow, 01-2861784

INNA
7 Old Dublin Road, Stillorgan, Co. Dublin, 085 142 0546

IRISH TEXTILE CARE SOCIETY
Rathfarnham, Dublin 16, 086 737 8737

ITS MADE FOR U
12 Newry road, Dundalk, Co. Louth, 042 935 7481

JENKINS SEAN & RUTH
20 Verbena pk Sutton, Dublin 13, 018391695

KINGS OLIVE
Vico Hse Main st, Finglas, Co. Dublin, 018641567

L FASHIONS
4 High St, Skibbereen, Co. Cork 028 51629

LARRY'S ALTERATION SERVICES
62 Main st, Swords, Co. Dublin, 018901525

LEE ALTERATIONS
19 Patrick's Hill, Cork, Co. Cork, 0214554779

LOUIS COPELANDS & SONS
Unit 30/31, CHQ, IFSC, Dublin 1, 01 829 0409

MARY'S SEWING & ALTERATIONS
Ballymacsimon, Kilmuckridge, Co. Wexford, 053 913 0926

MINEVICH STUDIO
195 Harold's Cross Road, Dublin 6, 085 111 4741

MOVILLE CLOTHING CO. LTD
Unit 2-6 Moville Business Park, Moville, Co. Donegal, 0749 385882

NIPS & TUCKS ALTERATIONS & REPAIRS
Castle Village Crescent, Celbridge, Co. Kildare, 087 2725374

OLGA'S ALTERATIONS & TAILORING
24 Lower Abbeygate St, Galway, 086 397 2578

OLIVE KELLY DRESSMAKING & ALTERATIONS SERVICE
Shankill Village, Shankill, Co. Dublin, 087 2718334

PADDYS CLOTHING ALTERATIONS
47 Nassau St, Dublin 2, 01 6714055

PAULINE'S FABRICS & DRESSMAKER
82 Parnell st, Ennis, Co. Clare 065 6828908

PREMIER TAILORS
Healthfield Rd Terenure, Dublin 6, 086 2284555

SAME DAY ALTERATIONS
61 Main St, Finglas, Dublin 11,

SEW ALL ALTERATIONS & REPAIRS
14 Rathgar Rd (Over Bombay Pantry), Dublin 6, 01 4975557

SEW CREATIVE
29 South Anne St (Off Grafton St), Dublin 2, 016359595

SEWING ALLSORTS
48 Cluain Dara, Knocknacarra, Galway, Co. Galway, 086 0701195

SHEILA'S DRESSMAKING AND ALTERATIONS
2 JKL St, Edenderry, Co. Offaly, 086 1744003

SHERIDAN SEWING
15a Thomas St, Gorey, Co. Wexford, 0539420156

SKERRIES FAST ALTERATIONS
86C Strand st, Skerries, Co. Dublin, 018491696

STELLA'S ALTERATIONS
Unit 1, Swans on the Green, Kilcullen Rd, Naas, Co. Kildare, 087 290 5531

STEVE'S SEWING ROOM
3 Main St,, Arklow, Co. Wicklow, 086 364 0774

STITCH IN TIME
3 Maine st, Tralee, Co. Kerry, (066)7119910

STITCH-N-SEW
45 Gardiner st Lr, Dublin 1, 01 8744653

TAILORING SERVICES
20 Verbena pk, Dublin 13, 01 8391695

TENDER123
Dublin Industrial Estate, Dublin, Co. Dublin, 01-4420614

THE IRONING BOARD
10, 11 Academy St, Meath, Co. Meath, 086 602 3443

THE TAILORS PAD
1st Floor, 76 Aungier St, Dublin 2, 01 4750853

THE ZIP YARD
8/9 Upper Abbey St, Dublin 1, Dublin, 01 8047419 www.zipyard. ie

THERESA'S ALTERATIONS
Lower Limerick St, Roscrea, Co. Tipperary, 050531718

THREADS ALTERATIONS REPAIR
Bray, Co. Wicklow, 01-2762132

TOP CLASS ALTERATIONS
40 Uppr Abbey St, Dublin, Co. Dublin, 01 8745037

ZIPPY ALTERATIONS
2 Henry St, Newbridge, Co. Kildare, 045 434713

*(THE AUTHORS HAVE MADE EVERY EFFORT TO ENSURE THAT THE INFORMATION IN THIS SHOPPING GUIDE IS CORRECT AND UP TO DATE.)

BRENDAN COURTNEY

IS A BROADCASTER, WRITER AND DESIGNER. HE SPEARHEADED THE RETURN OF THE BBC'S *THE CLOTHES SHOW*, WHICH HE PRODUCED AND PRESENTED FOR THREE SEASONS. HE CONTINUES TO PRESENT *THE CLOTHES SHOW LIVE*.

BRENDAN BEGAN HIS CAREER AS FASHION REPORTER ON RTÉ'S LIVE DAILY SHOW *OPEN HOUSE*. WHILE WORKING IN FASHION TELEVISION AND STYLING, BRENDAN RETURNED TO LONDON'S CENTRAL SAINT MARTINS COLLEGE OF ART AND DESIGN WHERE HE STUDIED FASHION ILLUSTRATION AND DESIGN.

BRENDAN CREATED THE INTERNATIONAL DESIGN COMPETITION 'WHO WANTS TO BE A MILLINER?' ALONGSIDE PHILIP TREACY AND STEPHEN JONES. THE COMPETITION CELEBRATES AND PROMOTES IRISH DESIGN AND EXPORT.

SONYA LENNON

HAS OVER 20 YEARS' EXPERIENCE IN THE FASHION INDUSTRY. WELL KNOWN FOR HER PERSONAL STYLE, DOWN-TO-EARTH APPROACH AND RAUCOUS LAUGH, SONYA HAS NOW BEEN PRESENTING RTÉ'S *OFF THE RAILS* FOR SEVEN SEASONS.

STYLIST, BROADCASTER, AUTHOR AND COSTUME DESIGNER, SONYA HAS RECENTLY ADDED SOCIAL ENTREPRENEUR TO HER REMIT AS SHE LAUNCHED GLOBAL NOT-FOR-PROFIT INITIATIVE 'DRESS FOR SUCCESS' IN IRELAND.

A PASSIONATE SUPPORTER OF IRISH DESIGN, SONYA HAS CREATED THE DAIS PROJECT, A TRILOGY OF FASHION FILMS TO PROMOTE IRISH FASHION DESIGNERS INTERNATIONALLY.